The American Housing Question

The American Housing Question

Racism, Urban Citizenship, and the Privilege of Mobility

Randolph Hohle

LEXINGTON BOOKS

Lanham • Boulder • New York • London

Published by Lexington Books
An imprint of The Rowman & Littlefield Publishing Group, Inc.
4501 Forbes Boulevard, Suite 200, Lanham, Maryland 20706
www.rowman.com

6 Tinworth Street, London SE11 5AL, United Kingdom

British Library Cataloguing in Publication Information Available

Library of Congress Cataloging-in-Publication Data

Names: Hohle, Randolph, author.
Title: The American housing question : racism, urban citizenship, and the
   privilege of mobility / Randolph Hohle.
Description: Lanham : Lexington Books, [2022] | Includes bibliographical
   references and index.
Identifiers: LCCN 2021039645 (print) | LCCN 2021039646 (ebook) | ISBN
   9781793636485 (cloth) | ISBN 9781793636492 (epub)
   ISBN 9781793636508 (pbk)
Subjects: LCSH: Discrimination in housing—United States. |
   Minorities—Housing—United States. | Racism—United States.
Classification: LCC HD7288.76.U5 H64 2022 (print) | LCC HD7288.76.U5
   (ebook) | DDC 363.5/10973—dc23
LC record available at https://lccn.loc.gov/2021039645
LC ebook record available at https://lccn.loc.gov/2021039646

To Henry, Gage, Maxime, and Shea

Contents

Acknowledgments

I wrote most of this book in the early mornings, before the sun came up and before my children woke up for virtual school, while chairing an academic department, in the midst of various shutdowns due to SARS–COVID-19 virus, in late 2020 and the first half 2021. There was not a whole lot of time for conversations and exchanging ideas with others about housing during the writing of the book. But I am indebted to a longer intellectual history and many ongoing discussions with scholars across multiple fields who have shaped how I see the world. Let me start with those that impacted my graduate training at the University at Albany, SUNY: Steven Seidman, Ronald Jacobs, Richard Lachmann, Nancy Denton, and Angie Chung. I was originally introduced to urban sociology as an undergraduate sociology major at SUNY Buffalo through Mark Gottdiener, with whom I later coauthored a textbook on urban sociology and continue to talk about urban development. Joe Feagin and I have exchanged emails about racism and studying whiteness for about a decade now. This idea for this actual book was originated in a paper I presented at the Urban Affairs Conference in 2019, so many thanks to Jason Hackworth and Tim Weaver for extending me the invite. There were many others, including Alan Shelton, Colby King, and Myron Strong, who have great insight into many sociological topics and are always a pleasure to exchange thoughts with. Finally, I'd like to thank my wife Rebecca for all of her support.

Chapter 1

Introduction

In October 2010 Jimmy McMillian, dressed in a black suit he bought for $99, accented with a pocket square made from a bounty towel, a homemade black tie, black gloves, and Karate shoes, sat on a stage at Hofstra University for a televised debate between seven candidates running for governor of New York State. His graying hair was slicked back. His white mustache, overgrown sideburns, and long beard made him look like a candidate running for office in the nineteenth century. Yglesias (2012) called him "a lovable crank born for the era of YouTube and Twitter." It was a brilliant presentation of self to ensure that his message would be remembered. A debate between seven candidates does not provide much time for a nuanced debate. On McMillian's right sat Carl Paladino, the Republican Party's nominee. Andrew Cuomo, the Democratic nominee and eventual winner, sat on his left. They both wore tailored suits. McMillian was an eccentric, but he was no polymath. He ran on a single issue, which he aptly named his political party after, that the rent was too damn high.

Although the media portrayed New York's gubernatorial debate as a circus sideshow, those three men, Cuomo, Paladino, and McMillian, embodied three institutional actors involved in affordable housing policy: the state, the real estate industry, and the people. Cuomo represented the state. As governor of New York State, he, along with the state legislature, oversees a network of state agencies that create the conditions for housing and real estate markets to exist. The Division of Building Standards and Codes regulates new construction, housing maintenance, and fire codes. The Division of Housing and Community sets rent regulations, enforces anti-discriminatory fair housing ordinances, manages the state's public housing stock, directs federal grant money to nonprofit organizations involved in affordable housing, and administers the Federal Section 8 Housing Choice Voucher program. Before

1

becoming governor, Cuomo was the Department of Housing and Urban Development (HUD) secretary. HUD administers key federal housing programs, like the Federal Housing Association (FHA) mortgage insurance; distributes community block grants to redevelop neighborhoods; and funds the voucher and public housing programs. Cuomo has had his thumbprints on housing policy for much of his political career.

The second institutional actor was Carl Paladino, a member of the elite real estate sector. The real estate sector includes a network of actors involved in constructing the actual built environment: developers, architectural firms, construction companies, and finance. The real estate sector is first and foremost concerned with profit. Urban political economists call the real estate sector *the second circuit of capital* because capital investment shifts from the production process, which is referred to as the primary circuit of capital, to the built environment during times of an economic crisis or when there is excess capital in the primary circuit (Harvey 1978). The political power of the real estate sector on the state and local level has to be understood relationally to the absence of national housing policy in the United States. U.S. housing policy is largely regulated at the state and local levels. The local real estate sector works with government officials to develop land and plan new housing communities. The federal government's role in housing development is to provide subsidies and tax credits and abatements through federal programs. The real estate sector is a very influential force in New York State politics. Not only do they collectively outspend individual donors on political campaigns (PAI 2019 Report), the state and local municipalities grant real estate elites generous tax incentives and tax shelters in exchange for creating new market rate and affordable housing.

McMillian embodied the final institutional actor in the housing market: the people. The people are aggregated into social groups like homeowners and renters; rich and poor; women and men; LGBTQ and straight; and Black, white, Latino, and Asian. McMillian was one of two Black men who ran for governor that year. Residents also have a stake in their neighborhoods and the economic well-being of the city. They form Community Based Organizations to fight for affordable housing. They form Not In My BackYard (NIMBY) movements to preserve single-family zoning regulations to stop the development and construction of new housing in their neighborhoods. They also form Yes In My BackYard (YIMBY) movements to deregulate zoning laws that interfere with building more market rate housing. Residents have some agency over the housing market. Through public hearings, residents negotiate with the state and real estate sectors on proposed development projects. Sometimes the state sides with the people over real estate interests. For example, New York State passed the Housing Stability and Tenant Protection Act of 2019 in response to the collective action of renters that claimed landlord practices of demanding advance rental payments, like first and last month's rent plus security deposit, and excessive application and broker fees were unjust. But overall, the state and real estate industry has more say over where housing is built, what kind of housing is built, if it is built at all, and how much it costs. Activists and citizens like McMillian continue to fight because they can't afford the rent.

The title of this book, *The American Housing Question*, is an homage to a collection of essays written by Frederick Engels in 1872 titled "The Housing Question," which were originally published in *Der Volksstaat*. Engels noted that the rapid pace of urbanization under industrial capitalism created housing shortages. The problem of low quality and unaffordable housing was a persistent problem of the working classes under capitalism. However, only when housing shortages affected those outside the working class did the question of affordable housing become its own problem. According to Engels, the real issue or question causing the housing problem was capitalism. Engels was adamant the housing question could not solve the social question of class inequality caused by capitalism, and thus, German workers should step away from social reforms and focus on eliminating capitalism. At this time, the German economy was going through a phase of rapid industrialization and capital investment. The German word *Grunderzeit* captures the rapid pace of industrial economic expansion of the German economy during its industrialization. *Grunderzeit* also refers to an architectural style of luxury housing built for the middle and upper classes in Germany. The poor and working class remained in tenements or working-class housing camps. Ironically, the installment of the series of articles attributed to Engel's *Housing Question* appeared in 1872, one year before the 1873 German Stock Market Crash that contributed to the global Long Depression of the 1870s.

At the back end of the 1870s appeared a text by the American political economist Henry George titled *Progress and Poverty*. Similar to Engels, George addressed the paradox between economic growth and the rise of poverty, especially how both were concentrated in urban areas. Unlike Engels, however, George saw a solution to the social and housing program through land taxation and establishing a belief in public good. George found that public and private investments drove up the demand for land, which drove up the costs of rents. George was less concerned about this process creating real estate speculation than he was with the creation of private monopolies over land and housing. Land monopolies capture rents and do not reinvest the capital into the inhabitants who reside there or the built environment, unless it is to secure additional rents. George's solution, which became the basis for a larger theory called Georgism that influenced the American progressive movement, was the single tax through land taxes. George argued that land taxes would redistribute money back into the community in the form of a

basic income, public infrastructure for inhabitants, and as an incentive for
landowners not to hold land for speculative purposes. A tax on land was made
in the name of the public:

> The complete recognition of common rights to land need not interfere, in any
> way, with the complete recognition of individual rights to improvements or
> production. . . . Everything could go on exactly as it does now—and still recog-
> nize the common right to land—simply by appropriating rent for the common
> benefit. (George [1870] 2009)

Unlike Engels, George understood the state's power to tax and redistribute
the surplus value created by capitalism back to urban inhabitants. He also
understood how a concept like the public or urban could be used to bring
together different groups under a common identity. For George, the public
did not conflict with private property. Rather, private property could be used
for the public good as long as it was taxed. The irony is that European states
developed public housing in the 1890s while American cities were beset with
privately owned tenements and slums that allowed landlords to monopolize
rents.

The American Housing Question takes on the questions and challenges
laid out by Engels and George and adds one very important addition: racism.
Racism, just as much if not more so as capitalism, defines America's contemporary social question. Much like Engels's day, America's problem of affordable housing became a problem when it affected the white middle and upper
classes. And similar to Engels's day, the problem of affordable housing and
quality housing is something that the poor, especially poor Black and other
racial and ethnic minorities, endure all the time due to residential segregation,
a criminal justice system that criminalizes poverty, and racial discrimination
in the labor market (Massey and Denton 1993; Wacquant 2009). Similar to
George, I hope to excavate the subjugated value of the public that has been
buried by American neoliberalism via a critical analysis of contemporary
affordable housing policy. To do this, it will require us to rethink the history
of how America approaches affordable housing.

You could say that our current policy to provide affordable housing is
not working. The prices of single family homes, condos, co-opts, and rent
have far surpassed what we would consider to be affordable. Housing prices
have increased in good neighborhoods and bad neighborhoods. They have
increased in coastal metropolitan regions, in the Sunbelt, and even the once
left for dead Rust Belt. There was a structural shift of capital from technology and the stock market to real estate following the 2000 global market
crash (Retsinas and Belsky 2008; Goldstein 2018). The cost of housing in the
United States increased 198% between January 2000 and May 2019 (Federal

Reserve St. Louis, 2019). The combination of demand side changes in mortgage finance industry and loose underwriting standards that expanded the number of people eligible for a home loan, and supply side changes, including consolidation in the home building industry and changes in local zoning laws that increased supply to historic levels, drove up the cost of housing. These changes in the financial and real estate markets led to a speculative bubble that resulted in the 2008 Great Recession and an excruciating halt to new home builds for a couple of years. After the recession, the supply of new housing modestly increased from the end of the recession up until the 2020 SARS–COVID-19 pandemic. However, a new round of speculative investors like private equity firms got into the landlord business. The cost of housing still went up. The increase in home prices along with increased supply of new housing throws a little shade on the idea that it is possible to just build our way out of an affordable housing crisis.

America does not have a national affordable housing policy. America's current strategy to deal with the problem of affordable housing is splintered across federal, state, and local levels. Supply side solutions, which argue that the only way to decrease the cost of housing is to increase the supply of housing, run into local opposition. Attempts to build new market rate housing and senior housing face stiff local NIMBY opposition. The federal government essentially stopped building public housing in the 1980s. They replaced public housing with the Section 8 housing voucher program. The need and demand for housing vouchers is so high that state and local governments shut down their waiting lists. What a solution! The resurgence of locals demanding rent regulations is met with fierce opposition from the real estate industry that sees it as bad policy that constrains the quantity and quality of local housing stock. In other words, for every solution there is a countermovement attempting to maintain the status quo. Affordable housing is a mess. And as I will show in this book, the reason why it is a mess has everything to do with racial-political context of affordable housing policy.

Housing policy sets the explicit rules that define the parameters of the housing market and the overall built environment. Affordable housing policy is a subset of housing policy that uses a combination of market forces and state subsidies to provide housing for the poor, lower, and middle-income families, and even upper-income families, in America's urban areas. The explicit rules set by policy are more popularly known as regulations. The two major types of housing policy regulations are zoning laws and land use ordinances. They largely determine what kind of housing can and cannot get built, and where it can and where it cannot get built. Zoning ordinances limit the height of a building and thus reduce the number of housing units. Local zoning regulations create a housing market around the much desired and maligned single-family home. Without federal or state subsidies, building

Chapter 1

affordable housing units is cost-prohibitive for local developers. The profits are found in luxury market rate units and large single-family suburban homes, which are out of the price range for many who need a place to live. Housing policy also determines the distribution of resources to different groups. Some of those resources are shifted to the poor via Section 8. The majority of those resources are shifted to developers. There are also implicit and unofficial rules to the housing market. They are found real estate practices that create racial segregation in spite of one's economic means (Korver-Glenn 2018), racial disparities in evictions rates (Desmond 2017), and the relationship between local elites and places (Stafford 2009). In short, housing policy is a conduit between the state and market involving regulations and economic funding.

This book is not directly about the limits of affordable housing policy. Rather, it is about how race organizes America's affordable housing policy. Specifically, I argue that the historically underlying logic behind affordable housing policy was to create the conditions for whites to exercise a right to mobility. In practice, this means creating the conditions for whites to find affordable places to live, for whites to have the option of homeownership, to allow whites to remain in desirable places. Because when we stop asking universal questions of whether or not a policy works, and instead reframe the question of who the policy works for, then a different picture of affordable housing emerges. My explanation is straightforward. When the beneficiaries of affordable housing policy were basically all white, then the state proceeded with a comprehensive and multifaceted plan to supply housing for whites, including public housing, subsidizing the construction of market rate housing, rental vouchers, and rent control. Affordable housing policy was not split between public housing and market rate housing. It was both. The white response to the growing number of racial minorities in cities and the civil rights movement fight to desegregate public life and institutions changed how whites viewed the desirability of public life. It was not that racial integration itself triggered an automatic movement toward deregulation of rent regulations, or enacted austerity measures toward urban policy, or privatized public housing. The white response to racial integration changed the meanings of private and public by associating private with white and public with Black (Hohle 2009, 2015, 2018). When we consider who benefits from affordable housing, we end up with a complex story of inclusion and exclusion and of privilege and mobility centered around race and social class.

Solving the problem of affordable housing means addressing that racism underwrites the logic of affordable housing policy, which transforms the right of mobility into a privilege, and is no longer capable of supplying affordable housing for ordinary urban inhabitants. In the book's conclusion I will lay out an approach to housing policy that embraces multiple features of affordable housing: public subsidies to increase the supply of private housing that is offered at 150% of the median income of a metropolitan area; the deregulation of zoning ordinances designed to keep lower-income, and by default, non-white groups out of white neighborhoods by prohibiting new housing construction; and the widespread use of Community Land Trusts (CLTs). It goes without saying that you have to increase the housing supply. However, we also need to address the question of why we devalue the notion of public and using public capital to achieve the common good. America has the fiscal capacity to solve the housing question, but does it have the willingness?

A POST-DISCIPLINARY APPROACH TO AMERICA'S HOUSING QUESTION

The housing question transcends academia's disciplinary boundaries. The reality is that the affordable housing debates sit at the intersection of sociology, economics, political science, geography, urban planning, and architecture. That is why I approach the housing question from a post-disciplinary approach. The larger point of post-disciplinary theory is to abandon a theoretical approach that searches for general concepts in the pursuit of a single grand theory to explain everything. In light of avoiding this pitfall, Steven Seidman (2016) outlined an approach to post-disciplinary social theory that focuses on debate clusters and domains. The focus on debate clusters means engaging the debates that exist around a particular topic or problem. It is a problem-centered approach rather than a deductive-centered approach to social theory. Deductive approaches are rooted in schools of thought that pit theories and traditions against one another. In a problem-centered theory, the evaluation of the merits of the debates shifts away from the hypothesis test to evaluating arguments "in terms that go beyond narrowly evidentiary criteria of scientific truth to embrace normative resonance, hermeneutic texture, and critical self reflexivity" (Seidman and Alexander 2001, 3). This is not a rejection of science or the scientific method. Rather, this approach also uses moral and egalitarian dimensions to evaluate social problems and solutions. This last point, considering the moral aspects of the solutions, is particularly important when dealing with affordable housing because it matters how much new housing we build and who we build it for. As Pattillo (2013) urged, we have to broaden our understanding of housing as something more than a commodity and also think of housing as a right. Although technical indicators based on aggregate data can definitely show us that a specific policy led to x number of new housing starts or the price of housing increased by y amount because of m, it does not tell us about the moral implications of these policies, such as how affordable housing policy was tied up with creating residential segregation, sprawl, crime, and capital disinvestment of entire central city neighborhoods.

Seidman's post-disciplinary approach also focuses on how a specific concept or process impacts a particular domain. A domain is defined as a specific arena of inquiry that forms around a social problem. The parameters of a domain are made up of the empirical aspects that define the problem. Affordable housing is a domain. It is a specific type of problem that is distinct from the domain of luxury housing. I am interested in how languages of racism organize the domain of affordable housing. By focusing on how race works through the domain of affordable housing policy, I can analyze what we know, like the racial disparities in affordable housing, alongside an analysis of the unobserved logic of affordable housing: granting whites the privilege of mobility. However, rather than apply a discursive analysis of race and policy, I am interested in how languages of racism are institutionalized in American citizenship that subsequently dictate the flow of material resources to those defined as good citizens. I will explain the relationship between citizenship and affordable housing policy in the next chapter. For now, I want to stay focused on the domain of affordable housing.

Affordable housing is a subset of the real estate sector. The real estate sector includes commercial and residential development. Within the category of residential development, we would separate affordable housing from the luxury housing market. The affordable housing problem is not something that affects just the poor. The federal government marks any household that pays more than 30% of its gross income on housing costs is considered as suffering from the problem of affordable housing. America's affordable housing problem afflicted about 38.1 million American households in 2016 (Joint Center for Housing Studies of Harvard University 2018). To understand why just increasing the housing supply alone cannot solve our housing problem, we can look to literature on housing and real estate from an urban political economy perspective. Urbanists interested in political economy and culture start their approach to understanding urbanization based on the premise that the dominant economic model of any given historical era creates its own form of social space that is conductive to its means of production (Lefebvre 1991; Harvey 1973; Gottdiener 1994; Gottdiener, Hohle, and King 2019). For example, industrial capitalism created the industrial city dominated by factories and housing tracts located in the central city. Deindustrialization and globalization rescaled the housing market across urban regions as factories gave way to office complexes, hospitals, and retail centers as the main forms of employment. The rise of the global finance and technology sectors associated with the "information economy" linked cities and their housing markets with global investment markets (Sassen 1991; Castells 2011). Housing costs and rents in coastal regions like New York City, San Francisco, Los Angeles, and Seattle have outpaced increases in the median income of their inhabitants. But so have the housing costs in Buffalo, New York; Orlando, Florida; and San Antonio, Texas.

Although affordable housing is a problem that affects all social classes, the problem is more pronounced when we factor in race and racism. Racism segregates racial and ethnic groups in spite of being part of the same social class as whites. Therefore, it is more accurate to say that the dominant modes of economic production and existing racial order create segregated spaces most conducive to the racial-political context necessary to sustain a class structure. Each racial-political economic system creates its own way to segregate groups and enforce systems of segregation. In part, it is because of the symbiotic relationship between racism and capitalism that created mutually reinforcing economic and political logics. The relationship between racism and capitalism is sustained by racial ideas, frameworks, and ideologies designed to reproduce elite white power across different historical contexts (Bonilla-Silva 1996; Feagin 2006).

Affordable housing first became a problem in America once it affected whites. The state began inquiring about the proportion of its population that owned their own home with the 1890 census. Collins and Margo (2011) estimated that the rate of Black homeownership was 7.7% in 1870, but grew to 24% in 1910, before declining throughout the 1920s and 1930s. Indeed, field research at the time, such as Du Bois's (1899) *The Philadelphia Negro*, documented how Black families took in lodgers, who were single or married Black men and women without children, because there were so little housing options in Philadelphia for Black urban inhabitants at this time. There was a sizable number of Black renters and lodgers who migrated from the south and moved from place to place, month to month, in search of housing. The federal government took action in response to the declining rates of white homeownership rates. In contrast to rates of Black homeownership, white homeownership followed a U-shaped turn, declining from 56.5% in 1870 to 43.2% in 1940 (Collins and Margo 2011). Starting in the 1930s, the federal government initiated a series of affordable housing programs designed to increase white homeownership rates. These programs included direct and indirect subsidies into the private housing market, such as mortgage insurance, public housing, and for a time, rent control. The relationship between racism and the second circuit of capital continued to remake urban America. Racial disparities in postwar homeownership rates and values became an intergenerational problem for Black America, a problem that creates racial sedimentation and acts as a barrier for Black upward social mobility (Oliver and Shapiro 1997). Segregation peaked in 1970, the same year that the majority of the American population began residing in the suburbs (Logan 2014). State officials and real estate development used racist discourses to define legacy industrial cities as bad and dangerous simply because of the presence of Black people (Hackworth 2019). Capital disinvestment of American's cities followed. None of these developments were natural, a given, or the result of individual preferences. They were created by racist affordable housing policies.

HOUSING FIELDS: REGULATIONS, ELITES, AND URBAN SOCIAL MOVEMENTS

The state uses affordable housing policy to mediate the relationship between the real estate sector, capitalism, and the built environment. In order to understand how race organized affordable housing policy and relationships that exist between housing markets, I draw from insights found in the concept of a strategic action field (herein noted as just fields). Fields are the building blocks for modern political and economic life (Fligstein and McAdam 2011; 2012). Fields are composed of multiple actors. In contrast to state-centered policy approaches (Skocpol 1985), institutionalists focus on how a set of enduring shared meanings and logics organize political institutions, instead of on the role of individual policy makers, to explain policy outcomes (March and Olsen 1984, 2011; DiMaggio 1991). Institutions reflect the collective interests of actors rather than the interests of specific actors. Therefore, the field is coercive in that its actors cannot opt out of the system of regulations, its cultural practices remain in place as new individuals enter the field, and rules and norms are enforced by the state (Bourdieu 1990; DiMaggio 1991). The logic of a housing policy field means that all actors involved in housing policy, including policy makers, developers, finance, federal- and state-level housing organizations, prospective renters, and homebuyers, share a similar interpretive framework to housing. While the various actors share a similar interpretive framework, they do not necessarily share equal influence over the housing field. Within a policy field there is going to be a dominant group who has the most influence over the field. However, dominant groups form alliances and cooperate with groups based on some shared objective. Race is the type of factor that binds real estate elites with ordinary residents based on the shared objective of maintaining segregated white spaces.

Under the framework of fields, affordable housing policy is conceptualized as a series of proximate fields nested under a single policy domain. Any given social arena is made up of multiple fields. Some fields are nested in other fields, some fields are proximate to one another, while other fields are distant. An example of a field nested in a larger field is how local housing markets are nested in regional housing markets. Proximate fields are fields that have some influence on the field under analysis while distant fields exert indirect influence on the field under analysis. An example of a proximate field is how a banking field influences a housing field via interest rates or its relationships with developers that results in an outcome like new housing construction. The typical example of a distant field is the state via its power to enforce zoning regulations. A parallel relationship develops between fields when two or more fields nested in a common larger field still function, but no longer have any real influence over each other.

Contemporary affordable housing policy consists of public housing, rent regulations, and subsidies for market rate housing. Although I use the term "market rate," this housing field is made affordable by direct and indirect state subsidies, such as federal mortgage insurance, state and local taxes (SALT) deductions, and various tax breaks and exemptions for developers. At one time, all three dimensions of affordable housing policy worked together as proximate fields when the benefits to housing were basically exclusive to whites. Public housing and rent regulations kept rents affordable as the housing supply caught up to the demand. The white response to racial integration of urban spaces first separated the three proximate affordable housing fields, transforming them into parallel housing fields. Although all affordable housing fields are distant fields to the state, the power of the public housing field no longer influences the private housing field, and vice versa. They exist as parallel fields. Over time, the power of public housing weakened via austerity and as it was privatized through vouchers. Rent regulations were also weakened over time as hard price caps were deregulated into soft price caps and decontrol provisions lowered the stock of regulated rents. The field of market rate housing was left to its own accord, charged by the state to supply affordable housing, but ultimately succumbed to the logic of the second circuit of capital.

Regulations

State and local governments use regulations to decide what and who goes where within a metropolitan region. Regulations set the rules and legal parameters of a housing field. Regarding affordable housing policy, the regulations of note are land use regulations that determine which type of housing can be built and how much housing can be built, in a specified location. Regulations include everything from the height of buildings, minimum lot sizes, minimum square footage of a structure, to whether or not a developer can build a multifamily structure or a single-family home on a particular lot. Other regulations include historic preservation that keeps old buildings from being demolished. Although racial zoning laws are no longer on the books, the spirit of racial zoning is still practiced through exclusionary zoning, such as minimum lot sizes and square footage on new housing, and opposition to the construction of senior housing and multifamily housing units in well-to-do suburban neighborhoods. The spirit of racial zoning ensures that the places where the majority of new housing is built, which is the outer suburbs, remain overwhelmingly white and wealthy.

Regulations exist within a field. Deregulation is the process of changing regulations to benefit one group in the field at the expense of another. There are social regulations that dictate safety rules at the workplace, offer protection from environmental hazards, and prevent discrimination due to one's racial, gender, or sexual identity (Vogel 1986). There are also economic regulations that provide the rules that govern market exchanges. In this regard, we have to think of regulations as more than just technical and legal administrative tools used by politicians and urban planners. Social actors work together to establish a normative ideal of the good life. They create regulations to help make this ideal into a reality. In practice, ideas of the good life reflect the interest of powerful actors. Housing and land use regulations correspond to dominant institutional logics that seek to bring about some form of order over economic forces. Within a housing field, a specific institutional logic informs how actors respond to housing shortages or increased demands for affordable housing. Their response is to configure the regulations within the housing field to determine the type and amount of housing supply.

It is a mistake to understand regulations as the state is trying to tame the market. The state versus market framework is a basic understanding of neoclassical economics, where the state interferes with and causes distortions in the market. Take rent regulations for example. Are rent regulations a form of capture-cartel regulations, which occurs when powerful actors act like a cartel and control competition and function like a monopoly (Schneiberg and Bartley 2008)? If this were the case, then rent regulations would exclude other forms of development but protect existing landlords who, even under a rent control system, monopolize the rental market. Or are rent regulations nothing more than price caps that hurt existing landlords by limiting their profits and provide a perverse incentive to skip upkeep on the property? In the state versus market framework, it cannot be both. Either the regulations benefit powerful actors or it hurts them. Once we abandon the state versus market framework, we can understand how housing regulations exist in relation to noneconomic objectives as well as economic ones.

Actors in the Housing Field:
Elites and Urban Social Movements

All actors within a specific field are aware of one another. One issue that arises in institutional theory is the problem of excessive determinism (Beck and Schneiberg 2005). Excessive determinism refers to the assumption that institutional logics and rules act as constraints to the extent that agency or change is not possible. Rather, institutional logics are partial or ambiguous, which gives actors the ability to apply the logic to fit their needs or wants. This is different from assuming that the dominant logic dictates an actor's needs or wants. Actors in the housing field have the capacity to reflect on the neighborhood racial composition and their normative idea of the desired resident. The logic of housing policy may correspond to a supply side or a demand side solution, but how the various actors enact or administrate that policy, which means enforce its supposedly race-neutral regulations, depends on the actors in a given field.

Who are these powerful and marginalized actors in the housing field? We can basically classify actors as falling into two abstract categories: elites and urban social movements. Elites are the dominant actors in the field. They include real estate elites, developers, planners, finance, professional real estate associations, and policy makers. What binds them together is a shared market mindset to housing policy and the access to the economic resources and knowledge to dominate the field. As I will explain in more depth in the next section, an emphasis on excluding racial minorities to protect property values and economic investment is rooted in shared racial frames and discourses. The shared cultural frames are just as important as their shared economic interests to make this a coherent group within the field. Elites use cultural frames to create alliances and cooperate with ordinary white residents, who enjoy institutional rights of mobility, and benefit from serving as the desired population for elite development projects.

The other actors in the housing field are urban social movements. Urban social movements are social movements whose form and claims are defined by their spatial characteristics. Castells (1983) defined urban social movement via their collective consumption demands. Collective consumption refers to publicly produced entities, such as water, electricity, sanitation, schooling, and housing, that are collectively produced but not equally distributed. Social movements can have direct and indirect effects on the field. They have indirect effects on the field by creating spaces for actors to introduce new discourses or new ideas into policy domains (Scheiberg 2013; Zilberstein 2019). They have a direct effect when their sociospatial practices create new forms of housing or change housing policy. Urban social movements can work with elites to secure housing or they can contest policy to bring changes to the field.

We can further break urban social movements into two subgroups. One subgroup is anti-racist urban social movement that demands inclusion into the built environment. Some scholars lump these actors together under a right to the city framework to capture how they demand the right to urban space (Purcell 2003; Harvey 2012). Urban space has historically been produced as segregated space. Segregated space corresponds to specific types of urban problems, found in the spatial dimension of poverty or crime. The root of segregated spaces is housing. Thus, addressing racialized urban problems means addressing the housing question. The freedom to live and move within urban space is determined by race more so than class. Anti-racist urban social movements like the civil rights movement, Welfare Mothers Movement, or Black Lives Matter challenge the racial basis of exclusion from urban space, be it directly through housing or the way the criminal justice system and policing enforces segregation.

The other types of urban social movement group are neoliberal urban social movements. These movements were created within housing policy fields that emerged after the neoliberal turn and focus on the private housing market. These groups cooperate with elites to produce or maintain a housing field that preserves whites' right to mobility in the private housing market. There are two main neoliberal urban social movements. One is the aforementioned YIMBY movements, who work with elites to increase the supply of housing or encourage economic development in urban areas (Brown and Glanz 2018, Shaw 2018, Gates 2020). They are often contrasted to NIMBY groups, who use existing zoning regulations to restrict the amount and type of development in a neighborhood. NIMBY movements support elite white mobility while masking their racism in the framework of protecting the integrity of the neighborhood (Nguyen, Basolo, and Tiwari 2013). The basis of exclusion, defined as the closing out of access to urban space, is the market for YIMBYs versus the state and market for NIMBYs. YIMBY movements are also different from urban social movements per Castells's definition because they demand a right to the housing market rather than a right to housing. All types of markets are organized around social relations (Fligstein 2001; Healy 2006; Mears 2011). Race matters in housing markets to the extent that racism shapes the social relations between buyers and sellers, renters and landlords, financial lenders and borrowers, real estate agents and their clients, and developers and local governments. Thus, housing justice advocates like Gates (2020) and Phillips (2020) stress the need to increase housing supply along with introducing tenant protections as the foundation for affordable housing policy for the twenty-first century. I will return to this line of thought in the conclusion. Next, we'll turn to a discussion of racial languages and how they matter to the American housing question.

RACIAL LANGUAGES AND THE DOMAIN
OF AFFORDABLE HOUSING

This book is about how languages of racism organize the domain of affordable housing. Now that the parameters of a housing field have been defined and explained, we can move on to what a language of racism is and how it works. A racial language involves both epistemological and ontological properties of racism. Racial languages create the meanings that organize and restructure relationships between concepts, which in turn define how we classify, define, and rank material attributes like spaces and bodies, as well as nonmaterial social statuses, like citizenship, that serve as the basis for distribution of material resources. A language of racism works as a metadiscursive framework within the domain of affordable housing policy. Racism influences how social actors understand one another, value neighborhoods, infer one another's housing preferences, and basically who benefits from social and economic policy. The presence of racism in a field means that we can assume that rights and resources are not distributed equally between whites and racial and ethnic minorities. Social science research on residential segregation has aptly shown African Americans endure negative effects associated with segregation, including how racism in the housing and rental markets maintain segregated neighborhoods (Massey and Denton 1993). My focus is on how different languages of racism dictate the meanings of public and private housing markets, the meanings of social and economic regulations on land use, and in turn, change the structure of and relationships between proximate affordable housing fields.

Racial languages situate the cultural meanings associated with a race in relation to the meanings of other concepts readily found in political and economic fields. We can see the use of relational understanding of race in Du Bois's (1995) concept of a double consciousness. Du Bois used the double consciousness to capture the way Black identities were formed as a relational process between the inside (the Black self) and the outside (white culture). Racial meanings are part of the social fabric of America, and social actors are consciously and unconsciously aware of them. In place of a binary, my relational approach to race is sequential. Each signifier maintains its associated meaning as it is placed in a sequence, rather than a binary, with an institution, organization, location, or policy objective. For example, a racial language like white-private takes the positive meanings "white" and links to them "private" in order to redefine the meaning of and social value of private. The positive meanings of white originated in how Europeans created whiteness in relation to Blackness, and subsequently functions as a generic and flexible white racial frame that gathers desirable cultural attributes under a conceptual umbrella of white (Du Bois 1969; Feagin 2013). The meaning of and how we value what is private is enhanced by its link to the racial meaning of white. Once cemented with white, private is no longer just contrasted to the notion of what is public. The meaning of white-private is relational to its opposite, Black-public. The negative meanings associated with "Black" devalue the meaning of "public." The concepts used within a political arena include the language of public and private that define the relationship between states and markets and the language of inclusion and exclusion that defines American citizenship. Thus, racial languages assemble meanings like white-private and white-public or white-private citizenship and contrast it to Black-public or Black-public citizenship which are institutionalized in political fields.

Racial languages are very different from racial ideologies. Racial languages create and sustain a given racial-political field because the order of and the relations in the field are dependent on its racial meanings. This includes dominant and subjugated knowledges and social categories and their relations with other social entities. In contrast, a racial ideology explains white social actors using racial ideologies to justify or rationalize racial inequalities specifically by denying that race matters. In this regard, a racial ideology, like any ideology, plays a supportive role in its corresponding economic structure or context (Bonilla-Silva 1996; 2017). Racial ideologies obviously exist at an abstract level. However, they are too abstract. The framework leaves us with abstract categories of a white state or a white market. An analysis of affordable housing policy through the lens of a white state or a white market does not capture the nuances of the shifting meanings of private and public that created different types of affordable housing policy and different forms of citizenship. An analysis that relies on racial ideologies creates a new grand narrative of inequality. It is a grand narrative that cannot account for contradictions and paradoxes found in affordable housing policy or rising inequality between whites. Racial languages explain why whites reject a racially integrated public in spite of the negative effects on ordinary white citizens. It also explains why whites do support using public capital or public resources when the beneficiaries are predominantly or all white even within a neoliberal political economy. In other words, my focus is less on proving the existence of racism and its role in reproducing racial inequality and more on racism as a social force that creates and reconfigures knowledge, cultural meanings, and values of nonracial entities.

Racial languages function as pretext that produces the competing logics within a given field. Policy preferences become regulations because powerful actors in the field can make and enforce the logic behind it. The role of experts and expertise is secondary to policy preferences. Powerful actors choose forms of expertise that support their existing policy preference. During his 1964 presidential run, Barry Goldwater consulted with the economist Milton Friedman because Friedman's racist economic theories reflected Goldwater's racist policy preferences. While some (Ip and Whitehorse 2006) have noted Friedman's call for a system of school vouchers to replace public schools as a key theoretical foundation that introduced neoliberal reforms to education, this was already a formal segregationist policy preference dating to 1953. Segregationist politicians in Alabama, Virginia, and Mississippi either privatized or created legislation authorizing local school districts the authority to abolish public education and redirect funding to segregated private schools in anticipation that the *Brown v Board of Education* decision would rule against them (see Hohle 2015, 149–197). This policy shift occurred before Friedman's then-obscure 1955 article on the distinction between government's financing and administering of public education. Prior to the *Brown* decision Black schools were not consolidated, received significantly less funding than white schools, and were run locally as private entities. School vouchers became actual policy in Southern states after the *Brown* decision, which funded the Citizens' Councils' segregation academies. It was not until 1975, after the political realignment of Southern Democrats to Republicans, when white politicians were looking to keep schools segregated for ordinary whites in a time of the racial and economic reorganization of American cities, did Friedman publish a collection of his writings on education in *There Is No Such Thing as a Free Lunch*. Experts still support, tinker, modify, and occasionally introduce new ideas into policy regimes. Nevertheless, we should be mindful that experts and forms of expertise play a supporting role to dominant political actors in a given field. Actors are initially influenced by pre-institutional racist or anti-racist forces and adopt forms of expertise to support their policy preferences.

White-Private/Black-Public and Proximate Housing Fields

Different types of racial languages correspond to different types of affordable housing policy. The racial language of white-public was the necessary pretext to support an American version of Keynesianism from the 1930s to the 1950s that used government intervention in the housing market to increase the supply and demand for housing. The language of white-public valued the role of the government to supply affordable housing, including public housing, but only to the extent that public benefits were restricted to whites. The language of white-public helped to create proximate fields that supported the public and private housing markets. This meant that changes in the public housing market had a direct effect on the private housing market, and vice versa. It also meant using government intervention in the mortgage and insurance markets to create demand and the conditions to increase the supply of private housing. Increased public spending on the public housing market also met the demand for housing for working and lower-income groups. Local administrators created segregated public housing units for white and Black residents, but that only created a Black-public housing field and a white-public housing field. The white-public housing field was still connected to the white-private housing market. Thus, the approaches to supplying housing via the public and private market worked well for whites.

The introduction of the language of white-private/Black-public in the 1960s and 1970s changed the relationship between proximate housing fields. Public and private housing fields are nested within a larger housing field. As proximate fields, changes in the private housing market created changes in the public housing market, and vice versa. The public and private housing fields became parallel fields after the federal government reduced its funding to and then privatized the public housing field. The language of white-private provided the interpretive framework necessary to privatize the public housing field. Elites initiated these changes at the federal level starting in the 1960s. Over the course of the late 1960s and into the 1980s, elite whites used the language of Black-public to justify austerity and disinvestment in the supply of public housing units. However, they initially used a language of white-private to introduce demand side housing vouchers to be used in the private housing market. In essence, the public housing field was split between Black-public housing and white-private housing market. Black-public defined the public housing projects. Once Black-public was embedded into the public housing field, the federal government defunded public housing to the point where it is no longer capable of providing affordable housing or affecting rents and housing prices in the private market. The language of white-private created the private housing voucher. Housing vouchers provided whites with a form of rental assistance that preserved the logic of white mobility. Unlike Black-public housing, the housing voucher was linked to the white-private housing market. Vouchers allowed whites to live in all-white areas because they could seek rental housing in the private market. But rather than checking rental and housing increases, vouchers only feed the market with rental subsidies. Because housing vouchers are set at fair market rent, which is calculated at the 40th percentile of all rents in the area, it creates a rental floor that artificially keeps rents high in areas that otherwise would offer cheap rents. The price floor works in the favor of landlords. Even if Section 8 was funded to meet demand, the price floor, combined with rules that permit landlords to charge rent in excess of the value of the voucher, are subsidies and regulations designed to ensure landlord profits and participation in what was the public housing market. Section 8 has the perverse effect of maintaining landlord profitability in economically distressed and often racially segregated neighborhoods.

Thus, the language of white-private/Black-public that emerged from the white response to the civil rights movement has had long-lasting effects on affordable housing. The language of white-private/Black-public transformed proximate housing fields into parallel fields. The Keynesian approach no longer worked once the language of white-private organized America's response to affordable housing. When the public and private housing markets existed in proximate fields, an increase in the supply of public housing should theoretically release some of the pressure off the private housing market that is experiencing an extraordinary uptick in cost because it is enduring a supply shortage, or if prices increased because of a housing bubble. Similarly, when the public and private housing markets existed as proximate fields, increases in the supply of market rate housing should siphon the demand for affordable housing from public housing and Section 8 and into the private housing market. Theoretically, an increase in the supply of market rate housing would increase the supply of available public housing or the number of housing units available for voucher holders. However, this is not the case. Market rate housing is built in the outer suburbs and is not affordable or accessible for middle and working-class people.

Languages of Racism, Epistemic Privilege, and Knowledge Regimes

One of the big questions surrounding America's affordable housing policy is why policy makers ignore alternatives given the fact that the existing affordable housing policies are not working. The way I approach this question is by analyzing the central role that culture plays in the field of affordable housing. Culture is what informs or shapes the informal rules, practices, and competing logics of a policy field. Therefore, my interest is in how ideas and cultural frameworks gain epistemic privilege in urban policy construction at all levels. Following Hackworth's (2019) approach to urban policy, this paper understands affordable housing policy as something that is often handed down by the state and federal government and as possessing an epistemic privilege that embeds a grand vision into policy goals. Epistemic privilege is created and maintained by knowledge regimes. Campbell and Pederson define knowledge regimes as the "the organizational and institutional machinery that generates data, research, policy recommendations, and other ideas that influence public debate and policy making" (2014, 3). Campbell and Pederson stress that policy makers draw from dominant or epistemic privileged ideas in times of uncertainty to "make sense" of a problem (Campbell and Pederson 2014, 3). Epistemic privilege and knowledge regimes create the normative vision of who should benefit from policy and are national in scale. Hackworth showed how epistemic privilege embedded in urban policy is more influential than either local self-interest or what voters or residents want. The reason why is that local interests or residential preferences are filtered through dominant cultural frameworks. This means that along with funding and legal mandates and other forms of land use regulations, urban policy involves a set of ideas that are imported into local contexts. There may be local variations in the type of affordable housing to the extent that local histories, economies, and housing markets vary. But local political actors will draw from the dominant racial language to use either the public or private housing markets to provide answers for affordable housing problems. Urban social movements make claims for housing through the same cultural lens.

METHODOLOGY

This book takes a long view of the American housing question. It is important to ground our understanding of how racism impacted affordable housing policy in the past if we have any hope of escaping the trap our existing affordable housing policies have placed us in. The methodology I used to analyze how racism organizes the domain of affordable housing draws its spirit from the Annales School of History and a more technical application from comparative-historical methods used by sociologists. Historical sociology measures change across time and differences within the same historical context to explain the emergence of large-scale social phenomena, such as the rise of capitalism, nation-state formation, and urbanization (Lachmann 2013, Barkey 2011). The formation of a social structure is understood to be salient, durable, and enduring into the present day. Historical-comparative methods align with the basic principles behind policy analysis: policy formation is historical because new policy proposals and modifications are based on real existing policy, and policy formation has to be analyzed relationally between the federal, state, and local level (Sabatier and Jenkins-Smith 1993; Quadagno 1994). This sets up an overall analysis between the epistemic privilege found at the federal level and how local actors responded to short-term crises. Historical sociology analyzes institutions in a historical context. For one, institutions are slow to change, and when they do change, change happens when the field can no longer adequately respond to problems or preserve elite privilege. In addition to stating how a given field or institution works, it matters when a field is formed. The timing of a field corresponds to a response to an outsider challenge or event. The inclusion of cultural variables, such as language, ties social actors to larger structures without negating their agency.

I also draw from the spirit of the Annales school because I want to account for how historically created shared meanings continue to shape decision making and social practices in the present day and to make the distinction between long-term and short-term histories. The Annales school focused on the long-term social and economic factors that drive history. This is different from focusing on political decision making or policy outcomes as the drivers of historical change or continuities. From this methodology, one places policy and political decision-making and even a broader political project like neoliberalism into its social and economic context. The point of situating policy into context is to uncover what Braudel ([1945] 1995) called the "submerged history" that is not always present or readily acknowledged by social actors. I don't want to reduce racism or languages of racism to something like an implicit bias, so I operationalize submerged histories as the ways racial languages are embedded into institutions, shape social practices, and the assumption that white actors enter housing markets with racial separation motives or preferences. This use of submerged history is consistent with the post-disciplinary approach to the use of the concept of fields and institutional actors noted above.

It is important to distinguish the long-term from short-term impacts of affordable housing policy. The economic goals of housing policy are more stable than the social goals (Kantor 2013). Tighe and Mueller (2015) characterized the long-term objectives of affordable housing policy as pivoting around the needs of the poor and creating the conditions for private investment. When we think about who the poor are and the color of their skin, the long-term goals of affordable housing reproduce the one condition necessary to attract private investment: segregation. The short-term affordable housing policy is the response to immediate crises. Any given housing crisis creates a short-term response. A housing crisis can be the bursting of an economic bubble due to speculation or it can be the racial integration of a neighborhood. Short-term responses are nested in long-term responses. However, we can still conceptually distinguish and operationalize the differences between the long-term and short-term effects of affordable policy by using a quasi-homeostatic analysis. A quasi-homeostatic analysis of policy emphasizes how external factors cause changes in policy objectives and settings (Howlett and Cashore 2009). This analysis measures policy changes through incremental or cumulative changes of a specific type of policy, rather than answering why one policy measure passed and another did not.

ORGANIZATION OF THE BOOK

Affordable housing policy is not doing what it claims to do. The simple reason why is that racism prevents affordable housing policy from working. However, nothing is ever simple. The complex answer is that racial languages have devalued how America views using public capital to answer its housing question. In turn, it has overvalued the role of the market to provide Americans affordable housing. The racial languages of white-private and Black-public transformed the relationship between public and private proximate housing fields into parallel fields. Public housing or vouchers no longer possess the power to subdue the private housing market. Perhaps

America will find the type of balance between public and private approaches
to supply affordable housing like it once did. That would take a new kind of
racial language, an anti-racist language, that once again values the role of
the public and no longer devalues sociological arrangements associated with
non-whites.

The next chapter uses a domain theorizing approach to map out the debates
pertaining to the American housing question. The chapter uses and rethinks
the notion of urban citizenship as it pertains to affordable housing policy. As
a social institution, national citizenship is embedded with racial languages
that create inferences of idealized or good citizenship. Even though urban citizenship is not defined by legal or illegal statuses, and instead pivots around
the status of an inhabitant, it is still nested in the broader meanings of national
citizenship. The institutionalization of different forms of good white citizenship created accompanying forms of affordable housing policy. Despite the
different forms of affordable housing policy, they all share the same logic
of ensuring that whites had the right and privilege of mobility. By centering
affordable housing policy debates on white-private urban citizenship and the
right to mobility, we can understand how affordable housing policy debates
have historically emphasized creating the conditions for whites to obtain
housing away from where African Americans reside. Affordable housing was
never about supplying affordable housing to those in need.

Chapter 3 begins the empirical and historical part of the book. It is an
analysis of affordable housing in the white-public era from the 1930s up
until the early 1950s. The original public and private housing fields formed
in relation to urban social movements, liberal reformers in large cities, and
federal policies that viewed homeownership as a key part of America's
political economy. Despite the involvement of social actors with different
economic and political interests, housing advocates drew from the language
of white-public to overcome political opposition from landlord and real estate
interests by restricting housing resources and subsidies to whites. Local urban
governments responded to Black demands for access to public housing by
offering a supply of segregated public housing. The combination of banking practices, federal mortgage underwriting practices, zoning and land use
ordinances, redlining and racial covenant clauses institutionalized racism
during wartime and postwar housing development. Segregation occurred
within cities and between cities and suburbs. Racial segregation created the
conditions for whites to exercise the privilege of mobility because both the
public housing and private housing fields granted whites the ability to have
housing preferences.

Chapter 4 documents how the elite white response to the Black civil rights
movement led to the undoing of the federal government's comprehensive
yet still racist affordable housing policy formed in the white-public era. The

Black civil rights movement had an underappreciated impact on affordable housing. The migration of rural Black migrants to urban areas changed the demographics of cities, the image of the urban inhabitant in need of housing, and reorganized the field of public housing. It was during the civil rights era of the 1960s and 1970s through an early neoliberal era of the 1980s and 1990s that the public and private housing fields became parallel fields to one another. Elite whites used the language of white-private to privatize public housing through vouchers, and rent regulations were deregulated to make it easier for landlords to decontrol their units. Despite the reorganization of affordable housing, it maintained its logic of ensuring the white privilege of mobility. The implications of creating parallel fields between public and private housing created a new kind of iron cage that carried over into the twenty-first century. Even many well-meaning policy makers and urban social movements cannot think of affordable housing outside the private market or the logic of white mobility.

The fifth and final chapter looks at the problem of affordable housing in the twenty-first century. The first part of the chapter traces the relationship between the language of white-private, citizenship, the role of globalization and the financialization of housing that originated in the 1990s. The second part of the chapter looks at current urban social movements and their solutions to affordable housing. It offers up a soft critique of two notable urban social movements today: YIMBYism and CLTs. Although both movements address different aspects of the affordable housing problem—YIMBYs emphasize the issue of increasing the supply of market rate housing and CLTs address the issue of profit seeking and speculation in the private housing market—neither address racism, racial segregation, or the logic of white mobility. In turn, I offer a solution is revaluing the role of the public by establishing a public housing field that uses a CLT model of bracketing out real estate profits in the affordable housing market to increases the supply of privately owned housing units in buildings, rather than single-family homes, complete with maintenance fees, and is dispersed across the MCMR rather than concentrated in the central city. We cannot solve the American housing question until we move beyond the widespread effects of privatization, which requires America to build a new political economy on an egalitarian and anti-racist form of citizenship.

Chapter 2

Urban Citizenship, the Privilege of Mobility, and the Affordable Housing Debates

The American housing question is tied to the question of American citizenship. National citizenship guarantees universal rights to all members of the polity. Rights grant individuals' legal protections from state power, set the conditions for an equal and just society, and the freedom to pursue their private interests. In the United States, citizens have political rights, such as the right to vote and run for political office, and economic rights, like the right to work and own property. These are considered universal rights. However, when universal rights are only enjoyed by a select part of the polity, rights become a privilege. Rather than a right to housing, the one constant across the different types of affordable housing policy is creating the conditions for whites to enjoy the privilege of mobility realized through obtaining segregated forms of housing.

The rapid pace of urbanization in the early twentieth century challenged the idea that citizenship was something that existed exclusively at the national level. The rise of the capitalist city and then metropolitan region created distinct spaces and governing practices for the exercise of rights and obligations pertaining to urban citizenship. Urban citizenship involves the right of mobility and the right to housing and shelter and access to other forms of collective consumption, including roads and a public education. In this regard, urban citizenship intersects with Castells's (1983) concept of urban social movements. Urban citizenship is more than a collection of rights at the urban scale. It also involves debates and ideas over inclusion and exclusion that define who and what counts as good citizenship. Good citizens enjoy the privileges of urban citizenship in relation to noncitizens and citizens that exist on the margins. To say that good citizenship is institutionalized means that the normal workings of affordable housing policy distribute resources and cultural benefits of housing to good citizens. It also means that marginalized

25

urban citizens mobilize through categories of good citizenship as they make claims for the right to collective consumption and safe and affordable housing. Racial languages are embedded in the institution of citizenship. They help to create idealizations of good and bad citizens that define America's national identity. America has historically developed affordable housing policies for good white citizens.

This chapter is divided into two parts. The first part of the chapter defines urban citizenship as a status nested within the cultural framework of national citizenship. I am concerned with a particular right of urban citizenship—the right to mobility—and how it impacts housing. The right to mobility is the right to move about the city (Lefebvre 1996) and includes the right to public transportation (Coggin and Pieterse 2015), the right to move about freely in public space (Sheller and Urry 2006), and the right to choose where one wants to live. Affordable housing policy restructured urban citizenship by converting the right to mobility into a privilege of mobility enjoyed by good whites. Racialized urban citizenship produced new forms of urban subjectivities, maintained residential segregation over time, and partitioned national affordable housing policy into a series of exclusionary affordable housing programs. The second part of the chapter situates urban citizenship and the privilege of mobility into the affordable housing debates. The point of the second part of the chapter is to familiarize the reader with America's historical and contemporary debates over affordable housing policy in order to show how a white privilege of mobility is embedded in the many assumptions, developments, and technical languages of affordable housing policy.

URBAN CITIZENSHIP

The concept of urban citizenship addresses how a common status emerges from this cornucopia of difference produced and maintained by urban areas. Urban citizenship is a status bestowed to all urban inhabitants: the rich, the poor, multiple racial and ethnic groups, multiple genders and sexual identities, and persons of legal and illegal statuses. Although urban citizenship is conceptually distinct from national citizenship, the normative basis of who and what counts as good citizens worthy of the benefits of urban citizenship is transposed from national citizenship.

National citizenship refers to the rights and responsibilities granted to individuals on the basis that they are members of that political community. The debates over who has national citizenship reflect the debates over national identity. This includes statuses of race and class and ethnicity and immigration that make up the domain of nationhood and inform the basis of nationalism (Fraser 1994; Kymlicka 1995). Nationhood is produced and then sustained by nationalism, the belief that a political community should be organized around a culturally based imagined community that ties all citizens to a common identity and destiny (Anderson 2016). How a country defines nationhood and the path it takes to state formation determines the form its citizenship takes (Brubaker 1992). Brubaker distinguished between a jus sanguinis or blood-based system and a jus soli or territorial-based system of granting citizenship. A blood-based system of citizenship determines citizenship by birthright. If your genetic heritage matches that of the state's dominant ethnic or racial group, one can obtain citizenship. For example, in Argentina, what it means to be Latin American was based in Italian and Spanish ancestry. Although it was originally used to distinguish Europeans from Indigenous groups and the descendants of Africans, contemporary Argentinians with Spanish or Italian ancestry can obtain citizenship in Italy and Spain (Cook-Martin 2013). The reason why is that those two nation-states have blood-based citizenship. The other system of citizenship is territorial-based. This means that one obtains citizenship by birth or residence in the political territory. In a jus sanguinis system, being born, for example, in Germany does not mean that one gets German citizenship. In practice, Brubaker notes that states employ a mixture of the two systems, where racial ethnonationalist cultures are intertwined with liberal and assimilationist models of citizenship.

We can add a spatial dimension of citizenship to the taxonomy of citizenship outlined by Brubaker. On the one hand, the very notion of an urban citizenship is that there is not a singular jus soli basis of membership. Nation-states define and recognize international territorial boundaries. However, urban areas provide another form of jus soli citizenship when local governments have the authority to oversee the distribution of resources on the basis of urban membership. This is what is meant by rescaling urban citizenship (Purcell 2003). In America, we find this rescaling in how city or county governments collect local property and sales taxes or distribute federal funding to build infrastructure and fund schools. Therefore, urban areas provide the actual sites for liberal and assimilationist models of citizenship to define the polity. On the other hand, the reality that America's urban areas rely on state and federal funding for housing and school funding means that urban citizenship is nested in the framework of national citizenship. While the distribution system is rescaled, the normative basis of good citizenship is not. And it is the normative basis of good citizenship that determines how distribution systems operate.

All countries have an idealized notion of the good citizen that underwrites or symbolizes the kind of citizen that reflects how the nation sees itself (Alexander 2006). Although American citizenship is a differentiated form of citizenship, where access to substantive citizenship varies by race, ethnicity, and gender, redefining who and what counts as good citizenship has changed the national and urban identity. On the national level, groups argue that they deserve rights because they are good citizens as they make claims for civic inclusion. This inadvertently reinscribes notions of good citizenship onto the polity, where being defined as a bad citizen emerges as the basis and justification of exclusion. For example, LGBTQ claims for equality meant being gender conventional and sexually nonthreatening (Seidman 2002). Black claims for equality meant being racially nonthreatening (Hohle 2009). However, the gender nonconventional or sexually threatening or racially threatening person becomes the embodiment of bad citizenship. These symbolic citizenship claims also entail the suppression of members who cannot or refuse to reflect the good citizen. As residents mobilize for affordable housing at the urban level, they make claims for collective consumption on the basis that they too are good citizens who deserve access to affordable housing and the right to mobility. In theory, urban citizenship grants one access to resources such as affordable housing based on a status of an inhabitant. This means that even though urban citizenship is nested in national citizenship, urban citizenship does have some autonomy over defining good and bad inhabitants. Yet the expression of difference via a group's claim to space varies. For example, as America has become more tolerant of sexual differences and extended legal citizenship rights to LGBTQ persons and couples, the historic gay enclave was remade as cultural archipelagoes, or spaces of sexual difference (Ghaziani 2014, 2019). However, this did not happen as African Americans gained new rights in the civil rights era. Even though a narrow slice of good Black citizens did move into predominantly white spaces, it prompted a white response and the formation of white-private spaces. Rather than Black civic inclusion reconfiguring the urban, what has historically occurred in America is the resegregation of Black America in suburbia and permanence of the inner city Black ghetto (Wacquant 2009). Race more so than any other social status serves as the primary marker of exclusion for national and urban citizenship.

My framing of urban citizenship as a form of political membership nested in a larger field of national citizenship differs from how others have approached urban citizenship. The literature defines urban citizenship in relation to the city as a political community composed of inhabitants (Holston 2001; Smith and Guarnizo 2009; Perez 2017). It draws from a broader perspective that transnational forms of globalization subvert the distinction between local and global, render the nation-state obsolete, and have centered global cities as the new primary political spaces (see Sassen 1991). The urban scale replaces the national scale as the primary political community because neoliberalism, economic globalization, immigration have centered urban areas as the main political and economic nodes of global capitalism since the late 1970s. Thus, debates about illegal residencies (Holston 2001) and inhabitants who define their right to housing based on the notion that they are responsible and committed residents (Perez 2017) make claims for legal housing on the basis of their urban citizenship rather than their national citizenship. Others have framed urban citizenship as an extension of Lefebvre's right to the city (Purcell 2002, 2013; Harvey 2012). Lefebvre's notion of the right to the city meant that the inhabitants and users of space should have an equal amount of influence over the production of space as governments and capital do (Lefebvre 1996). In contrast to these perspectives of urban citizenship emerging from the rescaling of urban or the framework of the right to the city, I do not see or find much evidence in the American context that the state has declined or that citizenship has been rescaled away from the national or that the city has emerged as an independent political community from the national community. The American housing question exists in a different racial-political history and context than the housing question of the global south. Therefore, I conceptualize urban citizenship as deriving from the meaning of national citizenship, which is conditioned on the dominant racial language, which in turn informs the urban inhabitants' access to collective consumption, such as affordable housing.

From the Right to Mobility to the Privilege of Mobility

Urban citizenship rights involve an implicit right to housing and mobility. Mobility refers to the movement of people, ideas, capital, material objects, and even nonhumans across spaces (Sheller and Urry 2006; Cresswell 2010; Sheller 2014). The concept of mobility rejects the assumption that places are stable or sedentary, and thus, understands the constant movement of people and ideas as a normal part of urban life. The movement of persons to urban areas, within urban areas, and between urban areas, including where we live and the physical and spatial connections between spaces, is how culture inscribes meanings into places (see Sheller and Urry 2006). Capital has always been mobile and one of the hallmarks of global capitalism is that capital moves between states, and switches circuits between production, real estate, and science and technology (Harvey 1978). This has not been the case regarding individuals. While America has no formal or substantive right to mobility or housing, both are institutionalized through housing policy and citizenship.

Mobility rights were just important for the formation of modern states and urban areas as civil and political rights were. The transition from a feudal to a capitalist political economy meant that one was no longer tied to the fields or agricultural areas. Breaking free of serfdom meant obtaining the right to leave and resettle elsewhere. Merchants and capitalists moved in between urban areas on trade routes and enjoyed special rights as urban residents (Weber

1966, 1968; Sassen 1991; Lachmann 2002; Cresswell 2013). National citizenship regulates and places limits on the right to mobility. Citizens are not free to move between nations without a passport or visa (Torpey 2018; Moran, Gill, and Conlon 2013). However, citizens are permitted to move about freely within the nation-state, but, like other rights, this form of mobility is a privilege enjoyed by good citizens. There is an important empirical distinction to keep in mind between mobility and displacement. The global elite and wealthy can move in between nations with ease (Bauman 1998). The movement of refugees and persons displaced from war, residents displaced because of gentrification or eviction, and the U.S. government forcing Native Americans off of their land are all examples of forced mobility, that is, displacement. Since the overarching topic of this book is race and housing, we will focus on how the privilege of mobility differs between racial groups, and its implications on housing and residential segregation.

The United States does not guarantee a formal right to mobility. The Supreme Court has ruled on mobility issues regarding the right to travel across state lines and upholding the Chinese Exclusion Act of 1882 to prevent Chinese immigrants from traveling to the United States (Cresswell 2006). Federal and local governments invest public capital to construct immobile infrastructure, like roads, cell towers, and housing, which lets urban citizens realize their right to mobility. It also creates the category of the bad citizen relegated to housing that dominant groups have abandoned, and spaces that capital no longer finds profitable. When these categories are racialized, the institution of citizenship creates good white, bad white, good Black, and bad Black urban citizens. Each category of urban citizenship is associated with a different form and degree of mobility. For example, racialized and deracialized institutional configurations of citizenship create the condition for whites to live almost wherever they want—even when they can no longer afford to live there. There was a steady flow of supply side investments in the private market to build new housing for whites to allow older housing to filter down to other whites. Not In My BackYard (NIMBY) movements nixed this flow to restrict new housing in in-demand areas, like Silicon Valley and Seattle, for whites like themselves. The exclusionary logic of NIMBYs forced middle-class whites to endure the affordable housing crisis. There was also a shift from a supply side approach of segregated public housing complexes that gave whites the right to not live in a slum to a demand side approach of housing vouchers that gave whites the right to live in segregated neighborhoods. The logic of white mobility meant ensuring that whites could move to different areas to maintain segregation or stay in place even when capital investments drove up the cost of housing and gentrified a neighborhood. In contrast, public and private capital retreated from areas after housing filtered down to African Americans. A housing voucher shortage emerged after racial and ethnic minorities comprised the majority of the population in need of vouchers.

Black America has never enjoyed the right or privilege of mobility. The right to mobility has historically been a white mobility that is linked to Black immobility (Hague 2010). For example, the 1850 fugitive slave laws required that whites assist slave owners who were hunting down their escaped slaves. It was repealed in 1864. In 1878, the Georgia Supreme Court upheld Georgia state law that prohibited Black landownership, while Florida and Louisiana had similar laws on the books (Copeland 2013). When prohibiting landownership did not work, whites used violence to keep Black citizens immobile. The overwhelming majority of Black America stayed in the rural South. Their mobility was tied to encampments of the working poor, for example, railroad camps, mining camps, logging camps, and convict camps. Whites responded to early twentieth-century Black migration to urban areas with racial zoning ordinances. Racial zoning ordinances emerged in cities with sizable Black populations, like New York and Baltimore, in order to keep Black residents immobile (Silver 1997). Rock n' Roll pioneer Chuck Berry was arrested and jailed in St. Louis, Missouri, for bringing a 14-year-old girl across state lines, which was a violation of the obscure Mann Act, but in reality, Berry was jailed because the girl with him was white. As cities gave way to metropolitan developments, whites continued to invent new police practices to prevent Black mobility. Late twentieth-century and early twenty-first-century police practices included pulling over an automobile for any minor and often made-up infraction, popularly known as driving while Black, or stopping to check Black men in the name of anti-terrorism and public safety, which was known as stop and frisk.

Privilege of Mobility and Affordable Housing Policy

The privilege of mobility is institutionalized through dominant racial languages, citizenship, housing, land use regulations, and state and municipal investments into infrastructure. Affordable housing policy sits at a nexus between all five. The federal government subsidizes and regulates housing markets to make homeownership affordable. It also provides housing vouchers to citizens, and if they are lucky enough to obtain one, to use them in the private rental markets. Some municipalities regulate rents. State and municipal governments create exclusionary land use policies and selectively invest in infrastructure so that only inhabitants of those spaces capture the benefits of public and private investments. Because white mobility and Black immobility are embedded into affordable housing policy, affordable housing policy produces and sustains racial segregation. America's affordable housing policy cannot solve nor could it ever solve its housing question because it does not address racial segregation or the underlying economic conditions, specifically speculation and profit seeking in the real estate sector, which have led to rising housing costs in periods of economic growth, economic decline, and stagflation.

A dominant racial language implies shared meanings between different actors is an affordable housing field. The languages of racism and mobilities work together in two ways: (1) they create new subjectivities and frameworks that define what it means to be white, and (2) they inscribe and erase racial meanings associated with urban spaces.

Mobility and Subjectivities of Whiteness

Racial integration changed how whites viewed and valued the notion of public and private. Whites valued public life, public spaces, and using public capital to improve the social welfare of the white polity as long as the benefit of national and urban citizenship was restricted to whites. Black migration to urban areas in the post-reconstruction era and then again during the interwar changed what it meant to be white and the meaning of whiteness in America. In the late nineteenth and early twentieth centuries, to be white was to be a White Anglo Saxon Protestant (WASP). White ethnics existed as a liminal point between WASPs and African Americans in that they were white without all the privileges of being white. Their white privilege could be characterized as a negative privilege in that it was obtained in relation to what they were not: not Black and not white. White ethnics' politics were racial and economic in nature. They only obtained economic gains and social rights by politically aligning with other whites. White ethnics were confined to slums and neighborhoods other whites abandoned. The main social movements of that era, including the populists; the union movements of the AFL, CIO, and the Wobblies; the Progressive Era; and the New Deal, were essentially all-white movements. African Americans and other racial minorities did take part in housing movements, and secured access to some housing, but there were so few of them numerically that it did not spoil the white identity. It was during the 1930s that the racial language of white-public formed. White-public created the racial-political context that supported large-scale public investment into American life.

What it meant to be white changed again during the civil rights era. Two social forces occurred simultaneously. First was the demographic shift of Black individuals and families moving from rural areas to urban areas. The second was that the civil rights movement successfully integrated public spaces. However, Black mobility to cities was often met with the realities of Black immobility within cities via residential segregation. Whereas white ethnics historically made claims to be included as good white citizens through labor (Roediger 2018), the white response to the civil rights movement redefined whiteness through the exercise of mobility. Mobility created real and symbolic distance between good and bad whites and good whites and all Black citizens. Good whites created real distance by moving to racially segregated suburbs and into majority white neighborhoods instead living in a white ethnic neighborhood. Good whites created symbolic distance through cultural tastes and social networks. Good whites could exist in the multiracial city or central business district yet never socially interact with African Americans and other racial minorities. Capital investment, in the form of housing, retail, light manufacturing, and professional jobs, followed whites to the suburbs and back again to gentrified neighborhoods. Understanding the relationship between whiteness and mobility helps us overcome the chicken-and-egg question over who counts as white: Is economic success a prerequisite to becoming white or is becoming white necessary to achieve economic success? By factoring in mobility, whiteness is defined through distance—physical and symbolic—from Blackness.

What it means to be white changed again in the twenty-first century. The changes in whiteness and non-whiteness emerged from the interconnectedness of the global economy through the finance and technology sectors. The rise of global cities acted as a pull factor for skilled workers from Eastern and Western Asia who entered the United States through I-9 visa programs. It also drew unskilled workers from Latin America to serve this new labor force food and clean up after them after they finished eating. Neoliberal labor reforms and social policy created the widespread feel of economic and racial precarity. These dual experiences of racial and economic precarity are properties of wealthy and upper-class whites. In turn, whiteness stressed economic success through the fetishization of the private and the market. One implication of the fetishization of the private is that collective action to demand affordable housing can no longer envision or support any action or policy provision that exists outside the market, that is, the public. Another implication is what and who counted as white narrowed to whites and those with light skin tones who were personally responsible and also economically successful, while what counted as Black expanded to include other persons and social groups with dark skin.

The defining of whiteness around white-private and economic success reflected the perception and reality that poverty is not a social problem for whites like it is for other groups. Economic precarity threatens whites' racial identity rather than trigger class consciousness. According to the U.S. Census, in 2000, the poverty rate for whites was 7.5%, compared to 22.1% for Blacks and 21.2% for Hispanics. Poverty rates increased across all demographic groups because of the 2008 Great Recession. The poverty rates for whites reached 13% in 2010, which was significantly smaller than the

Black poverty rate (27.4%) and Hispanic poverty rate (26.6%). Poverty rates dropped to 18.8% for Blacks and 15.7% for Hispanics, and 7.3% for whites and Asians by 2019. In essence, the white poverty rate stabilized around the 7% mark. Another way of putting this is that since 2000, approximately 93% of whites have not lived in poverty. To be white is almost synonymous with being economically secure.

Mobility and Residential Segregation

Racial segregation is a major way that whites come to learn and realize and practice their whiteness. A racial language is necessary for creating residential segregation. As a dominant racial language becomes institutionalized through the housing field, a distinct type of residential segregation will form within an urban region. The logic of racial segregation works with urban citizenship to create the conditions of mobility for whites to live and move in primary spaces while containing African Americans in the secondary spaces that whites no longer use or desire to live in. The initial studies on residential segregation, loosely grouped under the theoretical framework known as place stratification theory, explained that mobility was the outcome of social groups competing for social space (Park, Burgess, and McKenzie 1925; Logan and Molotch 1987; Alba and Logan 1991; Logan and Alba 1995). The theory explained that a dominant group will cede their claim for an existing space in relation to a subordinate group entering that space. In this theory, mobility options, the option to move or stay, are based on social class. Thus, the pathway for Black and other racial minorities to acquire the right to mobility is through economic gains, such as increased personal or family income, which will be realized through obtaining a home in a better neighborhood than what they currently reside in. However, a key question remains as to why would a dominant group cede control of valuable space when they could just as easily use political power to continue to exclude other groups? Another question is when non-whites actually entered white spaces. Was it before whites left or was it after whites abandoned the social space? Spatial assimilation theory cannot answer these questions. Institutional theories of residential segregation can.

Whites did not cede spaces so much as they created new ones for themselves. Historically, institutions have created racial segregated neighborhoods in American cities independent of social class (Massey and Denton 1993). That is, a middle-class income did not mean that a racial minority would or could gain entrance to a white neighborhood. The creation of housing fields around a given racial language means that the various institutions work differently for racial groups. Whereas whites experienced institutional privilege in housing markets, lending markets, and government policies like the mortgage tax deduction, Black and other racial minority groups faced institutional discrimination (Roscigno, Karafin, and Tester 2009; Korver-Glenn 2018). Because fields are defined by cooperation and conflict, what constitutes a dominant white group will be the outcome of negotiation and mutual interests, even if not all whites enjoy the full spectrum of the privileges of whiteness. Racism can create a unitary white identity by masking internal differences and tensions between whites because the benefits of whiteness outweigh any of the advantages found in multiracial organizing.

The privilege of white mobility gives whites the option to choose where they want to live, and they prefer living in predominantly white neighborhoods. White individuals, families, and prospective homebuyers all have racial preferences. Whites essentially cross off majority Black neighborhoods from consideration before weighing the cost of a home, neighborhood crime rates, or the quality of schools in their residential choices (Krysan and Crowder 2017). This exercise of the privilege of mobility is the power to ignore Black and brown communities and neighborhoods. Whites do not even think about moving to a majority Black or Hispanic neighborhood while Black families have to consider the economic costs and social risks involved in trying to move to a majority white neighborhood. The American suburbs became more racially integrated since the year 2000. However, Black suburbanization created an illusion. It appears that racial integration has increased on the county level while there has basically been no change in racial segregation at the census tract—since 1970 (Krysan and Crowder 2017, 17–33; Massey and Tannen 2015).

Once we get past the myth of racial integration told through the liberal grand narratives of progress, what we find is an ever-shifting relationship between racism and mechanisms to enforce segregation and Black immobility. For example, the language of white-public created residential segregation between city neighborhoods and between a city and its suburbs. This was done primarily through public housing and the initial wave of suburbanization. Public housing was segregated and used to solidify the boundaries between white and Black neighborhoods. Prior to that, the boundaries were somewhat fluid when whiteness meant WASP. Black families lived near elite white families because they worked in white homes. The language of white-private created new forms of residential segregation, such as the wealthy white outer suburbs and gated communities. These are places that have resegregated wealthy whites from ordinary whites. It also created new methods of enforcement: homeowners' associations, police surveillance such as the omnipresence of security cameras, new police practices such as "broken windows" and "zero tolerance" and "stop and frisk" and severe economic fines for minor infractions, and private security to protect private commercial property (see Davis 1990; Wacquant 2009; Hendricks and Harvey 2017).

The purpose of all these forms of surveillance is to mark desirable public and private spaces as white and unwelcoming to racial minorities.

THE PRIVILEGE OF MOBILITY AND THE AFFORDABLE HOUSING DEBATES

American affordable housing policy is a reflection of its racial-political context. In practice, this means that the normal workings of affordable housing policy create the condition for whites to exercise the privilege of mobility. Typically, affordable housing solutions are framed to be race-neutral. To uncover the racialized meanings of affordable housing we have to focus on how mobility is embedded in the affordable policy debates. Therefore, in this final section of the chapter, I will lay out the contemporary debates over affordable housing policy, including the objectives, assumptions, and overall empirical findings, and place them into their historical racial-political context. I want the reader to understand that a technical language created and defined by social scientists, policy think tanks, and government officials masks the racialized meanings embedded in affordable housing policy.

Supply Side Approach to Housing

The logic of the supply side approach is actually quite simple. In order to bring down the cost of housing, we just need to increase the supply of housing. This works on two levels. First, the law of supply and demand tells us that when demand exceeds supply then prices go up. The second is more complicated and has to do with the relationship between supply side investments and economic growth. This is where actual American urban and housing policy is important because the United States has historically pursued a supply side approach to affordable housing. According to Say's law that states that supply always creates its own demand, increasing supply side investments into housing will create a demand for housing and all of the jobs connected to the housing market. Basically, economic growth increases the housing supply and wages, and therefore, housing prices become more affordable via the ratio of income to the price of housing. From a policy standpoint, supply side investments include state subsidies into the private housing market to encourage construction. But what happens when supply outstrips demands? Following the logic of Say's law, it is impossible to increase supply without subsequently increasing demand. Unlike a style of clothing or a trendy toy, housing is not a commodity that we discard after it goes out of favor. We can never end up with an excess supply of housing, and increasing the supply of housing only induces economic growth and profit-seeking actors within the housing field. This is where the debate gets interesting.

Whether or not supply side investments increase or decrease the cost of housing depends on which side of the debate you are on. One side of this debate is how the shift in capital from the primary circuit of production to the second circuit of fixed assets like real estate and the built environment affects housing prices (Harvey 1978; Gottdiener 1995). This side of the debate understands real estate as a means of producing rents and profits, so the increase in supply is tied to increasing profits, not affordability. Subsequently, capital investment in distressed areas creates speculation and drives up the costs of housing. It has been the driver of land speculation and development in the suburbs (Gottdiener 1977) and the supply side aspects of gentrification (Smith 1996). The other side of the debate is based on what we may call the theory of housing inelasticity (Glaeser, Gyourko, and Saize 2008). A housing market is defined as inelastic when the demand for housing exceeds the supply of new housing and leads to increases in the prices of existing housing (Green, Malpezzi, and Mayo 2005). Housing markets shift from being defined as elastic to inelastic for a couple of reasons. For one, if we just look at abstract actors in housing the market, frictions can develop between preferences of homebuyers and the housing supply largely due to factors that lead to changes in demand, such as the preferences for the size of a house or the floor plan, or low interest rates (Levin and Pryce 2009) and policy changes that limit supply, such as land use regulations, building heights, and other local zoning ordinances (Glaeser 2019). Following the theory of housing inelasticity, the only way to bring housing prices down is to increase the housing supply.

Does an increase in the housing supply drive down the cost of housing? There does not seem to be much evidence to support this assumption. One study found constructing a large market rate apartment building in low-income areas led to a 5–7% reduction in rent in the existing housing stock in areas very close to the new building (Asquith, Mast, and Reed 2021). Unfortunately, a 5% to 7% drop in rent is not enough to make rents affordable. Nor does it lower housing costs or realign them with an individual or family's monthly income. Even from a neoclassical economics perspective, equilibrium only brings stability in the cost of rent and housing prices. Increasing the housing supply only eases the rate of its increase. Why? For one, stability in housing prices only occurs after a period of rising costs. Two, housing costs decline at a different pace than they rise (Glaeser and Gyourko 2005). An urban area that loses jobs and population due to a change in the business cycle or larger economic restructuring of the economy that pushes individuals and families out of an urban area will experience a decline in housing prices even if no additional housing is ever constructed. However, the second circuit of capital theory shows us that investment into the real estate sector follows the downturns in the economic cycles of other markets, like manufacturing and technology, so that even when the economy is bad and demand for housing should theoretically decline, it does not. For example, consolidation in the home builder industry combined with demand side banking deregulations in mortgage finance led to an increase in the supply of housing in the 2000s. The cost of housing increased. This was followed by the housing crash that triggered the 2008 Great Recession, which was followed by rising housing costs and rents (Haughwout et al. 2012). Furthermore, supply side investment in real estate has been an important driver of economic growth and tax revenue for local and state governments. The real estate sector accounted for 6.2% of America's GDP in 2018, a dollar value of $1.15 trillion. The commercial and apartment complexes subsectors of the real estate industry create distinct occupational categories, like the more than 280,000 persons whose occupation is classified as property manager. Furthermore, creating economic growth is not the same thing as creating affordable housing. Economic growth can occur and leave wages stagnant, which itself makes housing unaffordable. From 1960 to 2017, real median household income increased 49%, while the real median gross monthly cost of rent increased 93% and the median housing price increased 156% (Binkovitz 2019).

If we situate race and racism into this debate, we can see why increasing the housing supply does not automatically lead to lower housing prices. For one, white homebuyers basically only search for homes in white neighborhoods while Black homeowners are steered toward predominantly Black neighborhoods. In this regard, we may infer that racism creates racialized inelasticities within housing markets. As the vast sociological literature on racial segregation shows, homebuyers and renters do not know the market, but they know the racial composition of neighborhoods (Krysan and Crowder 2017). Whites only look at white neighborhoods with an existing concentration of whites that signal well-funded schools and urban services like snow clearing or trash removal, that are already expensive. Elizabeth Warren called this the "two income trap" because families overpay for access in predominantly rich white neighborhoods, and thus, drive up the demand and create an inelastic white housing market (Warren and Tyagi 2016). In reality, the two income trap is a trap for high-income white families who enjoy the privilege of mobility and will pay a premium to live in a racially segregated neighborhood. Black homeowners have historically endured an inelastic Black housing market. Black homeowners face racial discrimination in all points of the housing search. They are restricted to a smaller supply of housing inventory in Black neighborhoods or pay more to move to an integrated neighborhood. Racial segregation results from and persists because of institutional discrimination in lending markets and through housing policy like the mortgage tax deduction. Houses in Black neighborhoods are assessed at lower rates than housing in white neighborhoods, even when accounting for the quality of existing housing stock, amenities, and demand for housing (Howell and Korver-Glenn 2018). The real question is how do we untangle the supply side from the racial-political context of the second circuit of capital so that increasing the supply of housing leads to actual affordable housing?

Filter Down Housing

The supply side approach to affordable housing operates on a logic of filter down housing. Filter down housing refers to the process of when new housing structures are built, individuals and families will abandon their older and deteriorating housing for the newer housing, and the existing older housing stock will decline in value and filter down to lower classes (Ratcliff 1945; Bier 2001; Rosenthal 2014). Filter down housing works on the premise that the supply of housing will outstrip the demand, and thus it is the excess supply that will filter down. Filter down housing works with the theory of housing inelasticity based on the premise that construction of any form of housing, but especially luxury housing units that will be bought up by high socioeconomic status (SES) families, will lead to good housing trickling down to lower SES groups (Gyourko, Mayer, and Sinai 2013; Bluementhal, McGinty, and Pendall 2016). In elastic housing markets, the filtering down of available housing structures and units can work with demand side programs like housing vouchers (Rosenthal 2014). However, Mast (2019) found no evidence that new market rate housing filters down to the low-income housing market. The reason why is that the filter down hypothesis is rooted in another theory of chain migration housing. Chain migration housing assumes that new housing units cause up-renting. Up-renting is a process when high-income groups move into newer units and demand reduces down the chain. Mast notes that this theory assumes that a housing market is made up of only homebuyers replacing one another in the housing unit, where the reality is that housing is bought as an investment for vacation rental or as a second home. Therefore, housing does not filter down very far. Even in cases where new market rate housing does trickle down to lower-income markets, Mast claims that housing is already at its minimum and cannot go any lower. Low-income housing is also bought for investment or rent-seeking purposes.

It is not an accident that filter down housing focuses on the luxury housing market. As a pure market approach to housing, it is too expensive to build housing or apartment buildings with market rate rents without major government subsidies. For example, the national median cost to build a new house is $150 a square foot, but that price was $222 a square foot in California in 2018 (Raetz et al. 2020, 7). A multifamily unit that costs $800,000 to construct will need rents of $4000 a month to cover the cost of the investment (Raetz et al. 2020, 3). The costs to build housing in places like California have continued to increase since the 2008 Recession, and the new housing that has been built has not filtered down even to the white middle classes. Thus, researchers at Berkeley's Institute of Governmental Studies have suggested the need for more subsidized and unsubsidized housing, but even they doubt this will bring down housing prices or stop residential displacement in places like San Francisco (Zuk and Chapple 2016).

Zoning and Land Use Regulations and Deregulations

The failure of the filter down approach to housing has directed supply-siders to examine other barriers that restrict the housing supply. One particular issue is restrictive and exclusionary land use regulations that prevent new housing construction. Land use regulations that prevent the construction of new housing include zoning for single-family homes and height limits on apartment buildings and condominiums and historic preservationist movements that block development in the name of preserving the existing character of the neighborhood (Glaeser and Ward 2009; Glaeser, Gyourko, and Saks 2005; Glaeser 2019). The logic behind deregulating or changing existing land use policies is to allow the construction of new housing that will either be priced as affordable or increase the overall supply of housing units to trigger the filter down process.

The popularity of looking for affordable housing solutions via zoning deregulations is the result of the rise of Yes In My BackYard (YIMBY) movements. YIMBY movements formed in opposition to NIMBY groups, who historically were defined as any groups against the construction of polluting industries or social services agencies that help the poor from their neighborhood (Schively 2007). The YIMBY movement redefined NIMBYs as opponents of new housing units. YIMBY movements proposed market solutions to increase the supply of market rate housing to bring down housing prices. The concentration of the global technology industry in the Northern California region, the region that includes Silicon Valley, San Jose, Berkeley, Oakland, San Francisco, and points in between, was a significant pull factor for high-skilled tech workers and private investors. This increase in demand was not met with an increase in supply. NIMBY actors, many of whom were simply residents prior to the tech boom, worked with local government officials to stop new housing construction to preserve their property values in the name of the neighborhood's character. The YIMBY movement targeted the political issues of zoning, but it did not address issues of California's property tax laws, nor can it address the lack of a federal response to providing housing assistance or globally driven real estate speculation. The spirit of YIMBYism gripped housing groups across the nation in the 2010s. The reason why was that housing is not affordable anywhere. According to the National Low Income Housing Coalition, in 2018 there was "no state, metropolitan area, or county can a worker earning the federal minimum wage or prevailing state wage afford a two bedroom rental home at fair market value" (NLIHC 2018, 1).

What makes the YIMBY movement enticing to liberals and conservatives is that it embraces the private market as the solution to the affordable housing problem. This is not to suggest that all YIMBY actors reject affordable housing solutions like public housing or rent regulations (see Shaw 2018). What the YIMBY movement does is straddle the traditional left/right political distinctions found in the landlord/renter binary. In doing so, it reformed a housing field where local residents cooperate with real estate developers rather than view them as political and economic adversaries. The new adversaries were existing homeowners and municipal officials who wanted to maintain existing zoning and land use policies. At one time, local governments, real estate elites, and prospective homebuyers worked together to create exclusionary zoning ordinances. This included blocking development and selectively investing in infrastructure in already existing well-to-do communities (Trounstine 2018). Suburban governments and businessmen worked together to help developers acquire land for new housing and created zoning laws that stipulated minimum lot sizes and square footage of homes. These exclusionary zoning laws were designed to keep the poor and African Americans out of these spaces. This practice is still in use and explains why the majority of new housing starts are in the outer suburbs. By simultaneously targeting exclusionary zoning ordinances and working with supply side actors, YIMBY movements have reconfigured the institutional actors involved in America's twenty-first-century housing question.

YIMBY movements are both fighting to increase the supply of market rate housing and making a claim for inclusion on the basis of social class. They demand a right to the housing market more so than the right to housing. In part, YIMBYism exemplifies how the language of white-private redefined urban citizenship. YIMBY movements make an implicit claim that they are good white-private citizens who are responsible, did everything that they were supposed to do, for example, obtained an advanced college degree, delayed having children so that they could focus on their careers, and are not asking the government for anything, only to face a ruthless private housing market that betrayed its end of the social contract. In other words, YIMBY claims for inclusion are made at the expense of continued exclusion of others. Indeed, critics argue that neither YIMBY nor NIMBY are inclusive strategies for new housing because their appeal to market forces further institutionalizes anti-Black racism by excluding and displacing poor and minority populations from market-based housing solutions (McElroy and Szeto 2017). Racism and residential discrimination are the common denominators that link YIMBYs and NIMBYs. McElroy and Szeto (2017) noted that San Francisco's NIMBY movement arose in relation to the construction of wealthy white enclaves, but ultimately led to new forms of racialized developments in the region as capital investment still followed white neighborhoods. Similarly, YIMBYs still express racialized preferences for wealthy white neighborhoods as expressed through racially coded and market-driven aesthetic values, like Victorian Architecture, which drive real estate development and redevelopment schemes (McElroy and Szeto 2017, 16–20). Whereas NIMBY movements are designed to exclude, YIMBY developments are designed just to include good whites. Similar to other forms of affordable housing policy, it enhances the privilege of white mobility more so than actually delivers affordable housing.

The Public Housing Debates

The public housing debates refer to the best way for the state to provide housing and shelter to the poor. The contemporary debates around public housing are rooted in a moral question of what role, if any, should the state have in housing all of its citizens. If society's answer to the moral question is yes, the state should house all of its citizens, then the yes answer it generates a technical question: What is the most efficient means to provide housing to all of its citizens? In America, racism calculates the answer to the moral question and the technical solutions. The common threads through the public housing debates are to ensure white's right to mobility and that public housing does not challenge the private housing market.

Public housing was never a major affordable housing policy in the United States. Although public housing started in the 1930s, it did not become a notable form of affordable housing until World War II. Even at its peak in the 1950s, only an estimated 3% of the population lived in public housing. This was much different than Europe, where public housing has been successful in places like France, the UK, Austria, and Germany. Prior to public housing, the private market supplied housing for the poor in America. In large cities the poor were packed into tenements and single-family housing units carved up into multifamily housing units. It led to the formation of slums. The wartime housing shortages, followed by the postwar housing shortages, combined with tenants' rights movements, created a demand and a political context that ushered in America's public housing experiment. The original public housing complexes were built for white workers who paid rent to support building maintenance. Black-public housing complexes were separate. As the proportion of whites living in public housing plummeted during the 1960s, so did America's appetite for publicly financed Black-public housing.

The contemporary public housing debates originated from this racialized split in state subsidized affordable housing, and continue into the first decades of the twenty-first century. State subsidized affordable housing oscillates between the technical issues of *fixed housing* and *portable housing*. Fixed housing refers to the construction of large-scale permanent housing projects designed to house a significant number of people. Portable housing refers to offering direct rental subsidies to poor families that can be used to secure housing in the private housing market. Fixed public housing, which accounts for little over a million housing units, is no longer an affordable housing policy America pursues. America's public housing program is Section 8, which is the housing voucher program. The housing voucher program served about 2.2 million households in 2017 (Bell, Sard, and Koepnick 2018). Proponents of portable housing point to the time it takes to build new public housing and the cost of constructing, and then maintaining fixed public housing units (Zeidal 2010). The potential of portable housing as a solution to America's housing question lay in its relationship to the supply side aspects of affordable housing, especially the notion of filter down housing. There needs to be an excess supply of housing units and landlords who are willing to accept housing vouchers in order for Section 8 to work (Maney and Crowley 2000; Bell, Sard, and Koepnick 2018). Given that housing is not filtering down to the middle classes, solely relying on the private housing market is a naive and misguided approach to providing housing for the poorest Americans.

Even if it was the case that the supply of housing did filter down, Black families with housing vouchers still have to contend with the combination of classism and a racially segregated housing market. There are racial inelasticities in the Section 8 housing market too. The realities of racism prevent portable housing programs from working because racism nullifies the portable part of portable housing: Black mobility. Black families with housing vouchers find that their choice of housing is limited to racially segregated neighborhoods. One barrier is that landlords do not want to be in Section 8 rental market. Kneebone and Holmes (2015) found that institutional forces, such as landlords who refuse to accept vouchers and overall rental discrimination, steer Black voucher holders to low-income majority minority communities. Black families with vouchers, at best, can expect to live in a "low poverty" neighborhood opposed to a "high poverty" neighborhood (Sard et al. 2018). Landlords in segregated Black neighborhoods can charge rent higher than the value of the voucher because no one else will give rent to a Black mother and her children (see Desmond 2017). It is fitting that the success of the housing voucher is determined by moving Black children from an extremely poor to low-poverty neighborhood within racially segregated neighborhoods. An effective portable housing program would be one that grants Black families the same right to mobility that it grants white families rather than one that compares poor Black families with vouchers to poor Black families without vouchers.

Liberal proponents of portable housing tend to idealize and generalize the potential of vouchers to deconcentrate poverty by centering this idealization on the white privilege of mobility. In contrast, conservative opponents of fixed public housing use what Somers and Block (2005) called the perverse thesis, or when conservatives reframe the beneficiaries of social services as the victims. For example, in response to a renewed interest in public housing, Husock (2019) rejected any return to public housing because it "hasn't just been poorly executed: it's an idea with inherent conceptual and practical flaws. Those who suffer the most are those it intended to help: low income tenants." He faults the idea, but neglected to mention how the idea of public housing worked when it was adequately funded, tenants paid rent to offset the cost of maintenance, and the most important omission, when public housing tenants were overwhelmingly white. A new generation of public housing activists in large cities have mobilized around Public Housing In My BackYard (PHIMBY) and argue that attempts to use the private housing market to solve the affordable housing problem will ultimately end up making problems like gentrification and displacement worse (Mathew 2019). Although PHIMBY has not gained much traction under American neoliberalism, it does open up a debate on whether or not America should revisit a large-scale and national public housing project.

The Rent Control Debates

Rent regulations are a price cap on market rate rents. They are used to control the price of rental units, and cities or states have historically used them to stop landlords from increasing prices during a time of an extreme uptick in demand. Similar to America's public housing program, rent regulations, such as rent control and rent stabilization, were never a major part of affordable housing policy in the United States. There are no federal rent regulations. Only four states, New York, California, New Jersey, and Maryland, and the District of Columbia, have state-level rent regulations. All and all, only about 200 cities have some kind of rent regulations. What makes rent regulations different from the current housing voucher program is that rent regulations set caps on what landlords can charge. Housing vouchers set floors on how little a landlord can charge, so the landlord can still charge the voucher holder additional rent in excess of the value of the voucher.

Rent regulations are arguably the most maligned form of affordable housing policy by mainstream economists that exist, even more so than zoning regulations. The empirical studies on the effects that rent regulations exert on housing paint a different picture than a program that just suppresses the housing market and inefficiently distributes housing to those who don't need it. Because there are no nationwide rent regulations in the United States, any case study on the topic only captures the effects of rent regulations on a specific local housing market. However, we can still piece together some generalities on how rent regulations affect the rental market. The consistent findings are that rent regulations are effective at limiting rent increases, do not have a negative impact on the supply of rental units, and those with rent control or rent stabilization like it and tend to not move (Sims 2007; Ambrosius et al. 2015; Diamond, McQuade, and Qian 2018). In other words, it works as advertised. Research also suggests that rents will increase when rent regulations are decontrolled, which is obvious given that landlords will increase rents to maximize their profits. Opponents of rent regulations reject all forms of rent control for three reasons. The question is how much of this rejection is rooted in conservative ideology and how much of it is rooted in empirical evidence?

The first debate within the rent control debates is whether or not rent regulations negatively impact the overall housing market. For those on the yes side of the debate, the reason is that rent regulations are a form of price control that creates distortions in the housing market. Housing market distortions are defined by the gap between the marginal cost and average cost of housing. Distortions in the housing market prohibit the housing market from achieving equilibrium. Following this line of thought, rent regulations are an inefficient way to allocate housing because they benefit both the poor and the middle class, create fluctuations in the unregulated rental market, and lower the overall quality of housing (Gyourko and Linneman 1989; Glaeser, Gyourko, and Saks 2005; Glaeser and Gyourko 2018). Empirical case studies do not support this claim. In New Jersey, rent regulations actually increased the number of rental units because the regulations permitted landlords to subdivide apartments (Gilderbloom and Ye 2007). Why don't rent regulations negatively impact the housing market? The reason why, as J. W. Mason (2019) points out, is that unlike supply side barriers like land use regulations or the existing physical capacity to build more housing, rent regulations do not impact the supply of new housing in inelastic markets. As long as other market subsidies exist to increase the housing supply, rent regulations can be used as an effective affordable housing policy, especially in urban areas that are struggling to overcome zoning regulations. The real obstacle blocking additional rent regulations are institutional actors like the real estate industry who use their considerable influence over local politics to maximize landlord and developer profits (Gilderbloom and Appelbaum 1987). Thus, rent control is an effective form of affordable housing policy if the objective of the policy is to limit rental increases.

The basis of the second debate is whether or not rent regulations negatively impact landlord profits. Because this is the intended outcome of rent regulations, the objection or support for this debate is part ideological. However, another part of the objection has to do what landlords do with their profits: reinvest it into property via maintenance and upgrades. Therefore, a better question is "Do rent regulations negatively impact the quality of housing units?" There were a series of studies looking at what happened after Massachusetts voters voted to pass Question 9 in 1994. Question 9 abolished existing Massachusetts rent control laws. Glaeser and Ward (2009) noted that before rent control was lifted in Cambridge, Massachusetts, in 1994, rent control provided an incentive to delay or skip on maintenance because rental profits were about 20–25% below market value. However, Sims (2007) and Autor, Palmer, and Pathak (2014) found rents in Cambridge were raised in the same areas that were never subject to rent control. The real issue was that Question 9 allowed rent units to be converted into condominiums and that reduced the quantity of the rental housing stock. Landlords stand to make substantial financial gains from removing their rental units off of the regulated rental market, but only in housing markets with rising values. Neither study found evidence of the quality of housing going down. This is not surprising because other studies on landlord profits and maintenance found the same thing. For example, Bonneval and Roberts (2013) found that in the interwar period in Lyon, France (1914–1948), rent control affected landlord income but not maintenance expenses. Furthermore, landlords do not automatically invest their profits into their housing units whether they are subject to rent control or not. The New York City Commission on Costs and the Economy found that an increase in landlord profits in the 1970s led to a 30% decrease in renovations (NYS Division of Housing and Community Renewal 1993).

The final debate within the rent control debates has to do with mobility. In theory, residents have three mobility options. One, they can stay where they are. Two, they can move into a more expensive unit as their income increases or family status changes, what is known as up-renting. Three, they can spend less on housing than what they can afford, what is known as down-renting. Unsurprisingly, residents who benefit from long-term rent control are less likely to move than residents who do not benefit from rent regulations (Diamond, McQuade, and Qian 2018). The debate around mobility options leads to questions regarding the consumption of housing and its relationship to the problem of displacement. The overconsumption of housing argument states that rent regulations are inefficient because the middle class also consumes rent-controlled or rent-stabilized housing. From this perspective, mobility through up-renting is not just the desired form of mobility, it is the only form of mobility. Mobility options are related to the problem of displacement. Displacement is the negative outcome of a neighborhood getting gentrified. Diamond, McQuade, and Qian suggest that rent control inadvertently causes gentrification: "By simultaneously bringing in higher-income residents and preventing displacement of minorities, rent control has contributed to widening income inequality in the city [San Francisco]" (2018, 21). For one, this is not what gentrification means. Gentrification is a combination of supply side investment, the introduction of new demand side amenities, and the process of displacement (Smith 1996). More importantly, the presence of class inequality between high and low-income residents is an indicator that rent control works. In gentrified neighborhoods that have displaced low-income residents, you would find little economic inequality because there would be a homogenous population of residents based on income, educational attainment, and race. Rent regulations protect residents from displacement due to exogenous economic effects on the housing market.

Race matters when we are discussing the effects of rent regulations on mobility. Whether we are talking about up-renting, down-renting, or staying in place, the continued existence of residential segregation places real restrictions on Black mobility. Existing residents benefit from staying in place because it provides marginalized residents the opportunities to enjoy the advantages of an improved neighborhood (see Ross, Reynolds, and Geis 2000). Rent regulations have historically allowed whites to remain in desirable neighborhoods and entire cities during periods of housing shortages and rental increases. For whites, mobility is a choice that depends on changes in family finances, personal preferences, and other changes throughout the life course. The relationship between Black mobility and rent regulations is different. Here, context matters. For example, in New York City, you are more likely to find rent regulations in wealthy white neighborhoods (Ellen and O'Flaherty 2013). Black and Hispanics residents with rent-regulated apartments are located in majority Black and economically distressed neighborhoods in the Bronx (Furman Center 2017). Second, rent regulations have an effect on limiting landlord profits in places where they can charge rents in excess of the price caps. In neighborhoods that are not desirable, rent regulations give landlords rental certainty through tenant stability. For the landlord, tenant stability means that they typically have a good tenant, so they do not have to worry about the financial costs associated with turnover, missed rental payments, or eviction. Rent regulations also protect landlords from potential losses due to the bursting of housing bubbles or capital disinvestment. For landlords, there is a trade-off between additional profits and revenue certainty depending on the conditions of the local housing market. For tenants, rent regulations are a form of social insurance. It allows them to stay in the neighborhood, which provides neighborhood stability, and protects them from displacement.

In sum, the rent control debate tends to eschew the role of racism in the American housing question. Similar to the public housing debates, the technical language of price caps and regulations in relation to elastic and inelastic housing markets obscures the role of race in real and existing rental markets. When analyzed exclusively through a racially neutral lens, the debates around rent regulations end up pivoting around normative debates over the desirability and effectiveness of rent regulations over the housing market rather than providing affordable housing. The empirical studies show that rent regulations are successful at keeping rents down, but are not the cure all for America's housing question. Racism matters regarding rent regulations just as it does the private, public, and private-public housing markets.

CONCLUSION

This chapter inserted the concepts of urban citizenship, mobility, and residential segregation into the affordable housing debates. In doing so, it created a gap in the literature that explains why affordable housing policy does not lead to actual affordable housing. As discussed in chapter 1, all institutional actors, from prospective homebuyers and renters to financiers and developers, work under the epistemic housing policy assumptions that housing policy and housing markets are for well-to-do whites. What is missing from the affordable housing debates is how access to affordable housing is conditioned on the relations between good and bad citizenship. Good citizenship grants whites the privilege of mobility but only on the condition that Black citizens endure immobility. White mobility produces residential segregation, as whites exercise their privilege of mobility to physically and symbolically separate from African Americans. Since affordable housing policy only grants good white citizens access to a wide array of affordable housing options, affordable housing policy ends up creating racial segregation followed by class segregation. Residential segregation is not just a set of institutions that keep races separated. Affordable housing policy institutionalizes the privilege of mobility by creating the immobile infrastructure that organizes the placement of and connections between different racial groups. It also involves housing policy that creates new segregated places for whites to move to and creates the connections, such as roads, but also virtual connections that connect different persons to the workplace. Large-scale American suburbanization needed the car and the interstate highway system just as much as it needed the Federal Housing Association and redlining. The development of the twenty-first-century multi-centered metropolitan region needed the placement of cell towers and fiber optic cables just as much as it needed white-private spaces to allow high-income whites to traverse the urban area.

My conceptualization of urban citizenship solves the paradox between how globalization remakes urban areas and the continued importance and staying power of the state. Transnational links have changed the urban scale.

Without a doubt, large global centers connected by financial institutions and technology firms emerged as the centers of the global economy. The flow of immigrants, legal or otherwise, to these urban areas redefined what it means to be a citizen. Yet, the rise of transnationalism is dependent on the neoliberal nation-state. Subsequently, urban citizenship organized around inhabitants is dependent on the idealized notion of good citizenship embedded in national identity. In this regard, conceptualizing urban citizenship as an entity that is nested in national citizenship captures the dialectical relationship between the global economy and urban areas. Although white-private citizenship emerged as the embodiment of good citizenship in the neoliberal era, mobility rights and access to urban spaces continued to depend on one's racial or ethnic status. Wealthy urban areas are not all white, but whiteness still matters simply because it is institutionalized in so many economic relationships. Because good citizenship can only be realized on the continued production of bad citizenship, the exclusion of bad white and bad Black citizens is justified on the grounds that they fail to live up to the ideals of economic success and personal responsibility associated with white-private citizenship. Thus, as low-skilled workers flock to the urban areas in search of work, they find housing options to be limited, expensive, and depending on the region, confined to the margins or the inner city.

Understanding how and why citizenship matters for affordable housing means that we can rethink and reassess the affordable housing debates. Rethinking the affordable housing debates requires us to center the role of racial languages that shape the norms and networks of exchange and distribution of housing resources. Is it possible to isolate the rising cost of housing from its racial-political context? Once we get past the naivete of ideological dogma that we can solve social problems with market solutions and its ideological twin that the market causes all social problems, we can see that increasing the supply of housing is both vitally important and not enough. The reason why filter down housing doesn't work is that it matters who we build affordable housing for and where it is built. The worldview behind filter down housing is increasing the housing supply for high-income whites. In turn, housing justice movements come into conflict with NIMBY movements over land use issues like density and zoning, which are proxies for keeping African Americans and poor whites out. Developers propose to build new housing supply to meet demand, but they only build market rate or luxury units. Luxury housing does not trickle down to the middle classes, and developers are not building market rate apartments in distressed neighborhoods without generous state subsidies that socialize the developer's economic risk in exchange for masking the state's role in displacement.

Racial languages change how we understand and value public housing solutions. Not only did public housing come to symbolize the problems created by racism in the state and economy, the cause and effect relationship was inverted to blame public housing itself for creating the problems associated with public housing—problems that did not exist when public housing was white. If the housing question is in part due to the fixed nature of housing, then the right to mobility is amplified for whites because moving to places means they can distance themselves from racial minorities. Rent stabilization and housing vouchers work differently for different racial groups. Rent stabilization helps white residents stay in desirable and expensive and growing neighborhoods, especially if they add symbolic value to the neighborhood. In predominately Hispanic and Black neighborhoods, rent stabilization gives landlords income certainty. Housing vouchers give poor whites the option to move to suburban areas, if a landlord will accept the voucher, while Blacks are pinned to segregated neighborhoods in the limited supply of housing that accepts housing vouchers.

The next two chapters explore the history of how a unified field of affordable housing was created in relation to one racial language, only to be undone by a new racial language that ushered in the neoliberal turn in American politics. The shift from white-public to white-private citizenship is important because it altered the relationship between public and private housing fields. The relational fields of public and private housing were transformed into parallel fields where capital investment into the public markets, which have taken the form of private housing vouchers, public-private partnerships, and private equity purchasing pools of distressed housing, no longer keeps the private housing market in check. Combined with the profit seeking motives of the real estate industry and local and state governments using real estate to revitalize their economies, efforts to increase the housing supply end up driving up the cost of housing for all.

Chapter 3

Making Housing Affordable

America crafted its first comprehensive approach to affordable housing during the 1930s. It was a response to growing numbers of Jewish, Black, and white ethnic urban inhabitants conducting rent strikes to stop evictions, to stop rent gouging, and to secure very modest improvements in their living conditions. It was a response to liberal reformers pushing for public housing as a solution to improve public health and quell political unrest. And it was in response to a surge of urban migrants that were increasing the demand for housing far beyond what the existing supply could handle. Up until the 1930s, housing for America's poor was supplied by the private real estate sector, which balked at any notion of providing European-style public housing. Real estate elites worked with city governments, which took on an expanded and interventionist role in urban development. City governments began providing comprehensive public services, ranging from police and fire protection to libraries and schools to basic infrastructure like sewers and street maintenance, which increased the city's political and economic power over residents and capital at this time (Monkkonen 1988). The combination of the Great Depression and World War II intensified the housing shortage as the wartime labor and material needs limited the construction of new housing. It is against this backdrop of early twentieth-century urban America did the federal government craft its first national effort at addressing its affordable housing problem for good white citizens.

America implemented its affordable housing program during a time of economic and racial transition in its cities. The late nineteenth-century industrialization was the pull factor for immigration from Europe to the United States and for Southern Black farmers from rural to urban areas. The nation's urban population topped 40% in 1900 and surpassed 50% by 1940. Population increases did not just change the geographical size of

early twentieth-century cities. It also created a multiracial and multiethnic
city and an accompanied notion of urban citizenship that contrasted with
America's national identity. Urban citizenship threatened the taken-for-
granted assumptions of who and what counted as white in America. At this
time, the city was racially segregated by block rather than by neighborhood.
The development of the American metropolis segregated whites by social
class between cities and exurban areas that now make up suburbia. Indeed,
segregation by race and class increased 50% from 1900 to 1940 (Trounstine
2018, 26). It was during this time did the city and all of its spatially contained social relations become a distinct subject matter, captured in the rise
of American sociology attributed to the University of Chicago. In 1946,
famed Chicago School sociologist Louis Wirth called on sociology to think
about housing as a social value, how it relates to the community, and of
housing as social policy (Wirth 1947). In other words, Wirth charged the
discipline with viewing housing as a social problem that is both indicative
to a society's social values and as a significant cause to the formation of
cities. The social problem of affordable housing meant that there could be
no individual-level solutions to the problem because "an individual cannot
enter the housing market quite in the same manner as he enters the market
for other commodities as a producer or consumer, as a buyer or a seller"
(Wirth 1947, 141). Wirth was correct in equating solving the housing problem with the public interest. The question is "Who makes up the public in
the public interest?"

   Table 3.1 describes how elites and housing reformers drew from the language of white-public to create the domain of affordable housing. What was
distinct about the white-public era was how the U.S. government combined
a state-subsidized private housing market with subsidized public housing

Table 3.1   U.S. Affordable Housing Policy and Race by Field, 1930–1950

Time Period	Context	Racial Language	Affordable Housing Policy	
			Public Field	Private Field
World War II and Postwar (1930–1950)	1. Increased migration to urban areas 2. Wartime labor shortage 3. Shortage of labor and construction materials for housing	White-Public	White-Public • Public Housing • 1933 Public Works Administration (PWA) • 1937 U.S. Housing Authority • 1942 Emergency Price Control Act (Rent Control)	White-Public • 1934 National Housing Act (Federal Housing Association (FHA)) • 1934 Veterans Administration Act • 1935 Banking Act • 1938 National Housing Act • 1949 Housing Act

programs. Cities used rent regulations to offer tenant protections from rent gouging until the housing supply caught up to demand. In doing so, it created proximate fields between public and private housing markets. However, this arrangement was only possible because it racially excluded Black citizens from both markets. When Black residents fought for access to public housing, they received limited access to public housing located in majority-Black neighborhoods. Even though the demand for public housing among whites declined after 1950, this affordable housing arrangement remained in place because it ensured whites' right to mobility. In practice, white mobility meant the right to not live in a slum and live in a racially segregated neighborhood. As the next chapter explains, once the language of white-public could no longer guarantee white's right to mobility, a new language emerged and was institutionalized in affordable housing policy. For now, let's take a look at the origins of white-public affordable housing as it formed through Franklin Delano Roosevelt's New Deal.

IF YOU BUILD IT, THEY WILL GO: SUPPLY SIDE AFFORDABLE HOUSING

During the Great Depression and postwar years, America's main solution to the housing question was to build its way out of its affordable housing crisis. The reason why the United States pursued a supply side approach to build more housing is pretty straightforward. For one, the most direct way to reduce the demand for housing and affordable housing is to increase the housing supply. Second, there was an ample supply of cheap available land that developers could obtain to build entire communities. The problem with just looking at housing supply and cheap land ignores the complex political economy behind the state's role in creating a housing market that would not just build more houses, but build houses that ordinary people could afford. It also ignores the racist institutional factors that ensured that new and affordable housing would be restricted to whites, and the local factors that would create the conditions to enforce and make racially segregated neighborhoods. Finally, it ignores how a supply side policy worked in relation to other targeted housing policies, like public housing and rent control, to create an affordable housing field that supplied housing and bestowed on whites the privilege of mobility.

The state created the private affordable housing market. During World War I, the federal government worked with The National Association of Real Estate Boards to sponsor an Own Your Own Home advertising campaign. The campaign promoted the ideals of homeownership, specifically the single-family home, in conjunction with the ideals of citizenship through building communities (Lands 2008; McCabe 2016). Building off of the notion that good citizenship could be achieved through homeownership, the federal government began assembling a comprehensive approach to supplying affordable housing—to whites. The federal government used its power to set regulations to make the banking fields work with the housing fields. Specifically, Congress passed and Roosevelt signed the 1934 National Housing Act, which created the Federal Housing Association (FHA), the 1934 Veterans Administration (VA) Act, and the 1935 Banking Act. The FHA provided federal mortgage insurance to stimulate the nascent housing market mired in the Great Depression. The VA Act extended the amortization of loans to make homeownership more affordable and guaranteed the mortgages. The 1935 Banking Act provided federal funds to banks and gave the Federal Reserve Bank the authority to change interest rates. The banking acts introduced needed stability and liquidity into the housing market. Roughly half of all mortgages were in default by 1933 (Freund 2010, 110). This policy cluster was followed by the 1937 Housing Act, which provided federal funds for slum clearance and the construction of homes for low-income persons, otherwise known as public housing. Congress amended the National Housing Act in 1938. That amendment created the Federal National Mortgage Insurance, commonly known by its nickname Fannie Mae. Combined, these acts shifted the risk away from the banks and onto the government. Since the federal government does not actually lend money directly to consumers and would-be homebuyers, the FHA provided regulations over the banker's lending practices. Among other things, these regulations and lending practices created a racially segregated housing market paired with racially segregated neighborhoods.

In order to appreciate the housing and banking acts of the 1930s, it helps to have some context of what the private housing market was in the late nineteenth and early twentieth centuries. The private housing market was the domain of the white upper class (Radford 1992, 1996). Luxury housing and planned exurban developments were expensive to build but very profitable. Between 1870 and 1920, the affordable housing market worked through developers and investors turned landlords. The type of housing they built for workers and the poor differed by city. Baltimore, Philadelphia, and Albany, New York, had row houses. New York City had multistory tenement buildings. Chicago had two-story cottage houses, while Boston had its triple-decker homes. All were considered a step up from the slums. They were also overcrowded and cheaply built. The housing market changed in the interwar years. Harris (2013) showed how private developers and investors abandoned the affordable housing market after World War I. Although the increased cost of materials and labor increased the price of housing at this time, as did new building codes designed to increase airflow and let sunlight into the units, there was a broader shift in capital investment from tenements and row houses and triplexes to large planned communities on the outskirts of the city. Thus, there was an already affordable housing crisis leading up to the Depression and World War II. The war and depression amplified the affordable housing problem, but they did not cause it. After 1920, the single-family residence became the standard type of housing structure built for America's white middle class.

As developers abandoned building affordable housing for the poor in favor of luxury housing and planned developments, they institutionalized filter down affordable housing policy. Filtering down meant building housing for the rich, who would move on from neighborhoods or their existing deteriorating housing units, in favor of new housing, buildings, and planned communities. Harris (2012) showed that the idea of filter down housing became the de facto housing policy at this time, and has persisted as a fundamental assumption on market approaches to housing policy ever since. The logic of filter down housing institutionalized the privilege of mobility for whites. While wealthy whites always enjoyed the right of mobility, it was the market's expansion into single-family homes and suburban development that extended the privilege of mobility to the white middle class. It was public housing, not the private market, that granted the working class and poor whites the privilege of mobility.

The racial language of white-public organized the field of affordable housing policy. A field is made up of multiple social actors. White-public provided the logic to coordinate the various actors, like a conductor guiding an orchestra. These social actors drew from existing racist practices to create and then maintain segregated neighborhoods while ensuring that the benefits and resources of urban citizenship were reserved for whites. For example, cities began using the power of zoning in the early 1900s. Zoning was originally intended for determining how land should be used, such as keeping factories away from residential areas. Cities with notable Black populations, which was rare given that approximately 80% of the Black population lived in rural areas at this time, were the places that implemented racial zoning ordinances (Silver 1997). Racial zoning ordinances differed by city, as some cities were racially zoned by block while others zoned by ward or district. Racial zoning ordinances made it illegal for Black families to purchase homes and reside in majority white neighborhoods. At the turn of the twentieth century, a Black neighborhood was likely to be an integrated neighborhood (Du Bois 1899; Shaw and McKay 1942). Racial zoning tended to appear in cities that had a Black community with some economic power and political clout. This included the cities in the upper south that bordered the Mason-Dixon Line or on the Mississippi River, from New Orleans to Louisville to Baltimore, as well as New York City, Birmingham, Alabama, and Atlanta, Georgia. The Supreme Court ruled that racial zoning was

unconstitutional in the 1917 *Buchanan v. Warley* case. The ruling was not
based on protecting the rights of Black families. It was based on protecting
the rights of white homeowners to sell their homes to whomever they wanted
to (Rothstein 2017, 45).

Although racial zoning was deemed illegal,[1] the spirit of racial zoning continued through white-public institutional practices. The spirit of racial zoning refers
to how a language of racism was embedded in everyday administrative and
economic exchanges involved in creating a racially segregated private housing
market. There were two institutional-level practices of note at this time: racial
covenants and redlining. The result was the most significant form of human
settlement space in the twentieth century, suburbanization. More than any other
aspects of affordable housing policy, mid-twentieth-century suburbanization
created the conditions for whites to exercise their privilege of mobility.

The political and financial viability of building private sector affordable
homes and communities depended on them being racially segregated. White
bankers and developers worked together to ensure that federally backed
and insured mortgages were directed to prospective white homebuyers in
white communities. They followed FHA guidelines and defined the presence of "undesirable racial or nationality groups" as a factor to deny federal
mortgage insurance. The practice of redlining started with the government-
backed Home Owners Loan Corporation (HOLC) in the 1930s. Once the
FHA adopted redlining and made it a part of their underwriting guidelines,
redlining became an institutional practice of the private affordable housing
market. Redlining was named after the ways that banks drew green lines on
a map around the neighborhoods that they would lend money to and drew
red lines around neighborhoods they would not. Mortgages that did qualify
for FHA insurance had higher interest rates. Between 1940 and 1960, racial
segregation increased in places that HOLC conducted appraisals, and places
that underwent HOLC appraisals were more segregated than places that the
HOLC did not appraise (Faber 2020). Given that only 2% of all FHA loans
went to racial minorities (Leighninger, Jr. 2007), Black families paid a higher
interest on mortgage for a house that was more expensive and quickly became
a depreciating asset than houses purchased by whites. Racism in the job market created an income gap between whites and Blacks, so the mortgage and
other costs associated with homeownership ate up more of a Black family's
monthly budget. In turn, many Black homeowners became landlords and
Black neighborhoods became overcrowded. White homeowners, on the other
hand, faced none of this institutional discrimination, and enjoyed fully funded
and racially segregated public amenities (Hohle 2018, 138–146)

A second way that bankers and developers collaborated to maintain racial
segregation in the private affordable housing market was through the restrictive covenant, more popularly known as a racial covenant. A restrictive

covenant is a clause inserted into a housing deed that places restrictions on what the homeowners can do to the exterior of the home. However, they were known as racial covenants because the primary clause in the deed was that it prohibited a white homeowner from selling their home to a Black person or family. This embedded racism into a basic economic exchange at the level of the contract. On their own, a racial covenant was an ineffective means of maintaining racial segregation. The injured party was the original owner who sold the house, who no longer had an interest in the community (Rothstein 2017, 79). Developers came up with a solution. They created community associations with a racial covenant clause that were part of the community itself. The injured party was now the community. Whereas racial zoning was tied with the financial sector and government policy, the racial covenant clauses were directly tied to private economy. White developers and homeowners took personal and communal responsibility for creating and maintaining racial segregation within the market itself. Combined, the FHA and federal banking acts created the conditions for the establishment of the racially segregated private affordable housing market, which white developers, politicians, and homeowners maintained through private contracts and community associations.

Suburbanization was the pinnacle of the market solutions to affordable housing. The combination of federal housing and banking policy with the spirit of racial zoning created the conditions for the state and developers to increase the supply of affordable housing for whites. The availability of cheap land meant that space was available to build entire all-white communities. The term "white flight" captures how whites fled cities for the surrounding suburbs. White flight was simply the realization of the white privilege of mobility. It was a privilege that created a nation of white homeowners, and for the first time in American history, the creation of wealth for the white working class.

The language of white-public associated public goods and services as white-public capital. Public capital refers to the use of public financial resources, such as direct and indirect subsidies, including but not limited to tax abatements, tax credits, and direct expenditures into the built environment. White-public capital was deployed in the interest of white-private capital, especially as it pertained to housing and the real estate sector. As long as the racial interests of capital were met, there was little resistance to whites using state power to increase the supply of private homes. Whites readily believed that they were the only ones who paid taxes, a belief that was as prominent in the early twentieth century as it is in the early twenty-first century (Hohle 2015, 68–71, 95–102). This was especially true of white homeowners and landlords who paid property taxes. During the 1930s, city and suburban governments worked with wealthy white homeowners to implement land use regulations to ensure that white homeowners captured public services (Trounstine 2018).

White homeowner associations fought against open housing laws, against their white neighbors from selling their homes to Blacks families, and against the placement of public housing near their homes (Kruse 2005). Racial segregation existed before the advent of public housing, although the racial segregation of public amenities—like schools and housing—firmed up the racially segregated neighborhood boundaries. The cooperation between the real estate sector and the state to increase the supply of affordable housing was built on the existing racialized practices that affordable housing was only culturally and financially feasible as long as it was racially segregated.

Developers had to create a normative meaning of suburban life as superior to city living. Only 15% of Americans lived in the suburbs in 1940. The meaning of suburban life, or what was then called exurban communities, was not automatically viewed as superior to city life. As Gottdiener noted, cities were considered decent places to live, but that "Suburban relocation developed into a mass movement primarily as a consequence of attractive supply-side features made available to the majority of its citizens, who happened to be white" (1995, 10). The supply side features made suburban life cost-effective for the working and middle classes. However, it was the cultural and demand side features of suburban life that created a racial dichotomy between the suburb and the city. Suburban developers used the spirit of racial zoning. Suburban life was made superior to city living by offering racially segregated and fully funded public amenities. The courts supported the legal exclusion of Black families from suburban development. Racial covenant clauses were inserted into deeds. Suburban governments also introduced distinct forms of zoning into the suburbs, such as single-family zoning and exclusionary zoning. Single-family zoning prohibited the construction of doubles and apartment buildings. This meant that the affordable private housing was limited to homeownership. Exclusionary zoning meant low-density land use. Low-density land use was achieved through land use policies that mandated larger lot sizes, more room between houses, and eventually increased the minimal square footage of the home. If place stratification theory was correct, then middle- and upper-income Black families should have been able to move into the suburbs. They were not. It was the institutionalization of racism into all aspects of the private affordable housing market that solved the housing question for whites.

PUBLIC HOUSING AND THE WHITE PRIVILEGE TO NOT LIVE IN SLUMS

The white-public era created the conditions for all aspects of affordable housing to work together. Whereas the private affordable housing market increased the supply of market rate affordable homes for middle- and upper-income whites, white-public housing supplied housing for working-class and low-income whites. They both were racially segregated. They both granted whites the privilege of mobility. In the case of public housing, it was the privilege of whites living in big cities to no longer reside in slums or tenements. Public housing was designed to work with the supply side efforts to build more housing in the private market. It was intended to house working-class whites who could pay some form of rent to cover the cost of maintenance. Because the public and private housing fields existed as proximate fields, the public and private housing market worked together to solve the affordable housing problem for whites by the end of the 1940s and early 1950s.

The federal government first experimented with public housing during World War I. They built housing for factory workers who migrated to places where firms who contracted with the defense industry were located. A total of 83 housing projects were built to house roughly 170,000 families (Rothstein 2017, 18). However, Marcuse ([1978] 2016) notes that because the defense industries were located in factory towns, these public housing provisions were created to meet the needs of the defense industry and not as a real form of affordable housing. The defense industry housing projects were designed to be temporary accommodations. The federal government mandated that the housing was sold to private developers at the conclusion of the war. The housing units were also restricted to whites. Black workers were forced to live on the outskirts of town, sometimes in tents, and other times in shacks. This was a very limited supply of public housing. As noted earlier, the vast majority of the poor and working class lived in privately owned rental housing.

Public housing was not a blessing from elites onto the poor. It was an elite response to the unrest among the growing ranks of the poor. A series of rent strikes appeared in large U.S. cities in the early 1930s. Private landlords owned the structures that housed the poor. The Depression increased unemployment, and the absence of any protective legislation or housing policy for renters allowed landlords to increase rents and evict as they desired. Rent riots and rent strikes appeared in New York's Lower East Side and Harlem neighborhoods, where unemployment was the highest, and in Chicago's Black neighborhoods, where the levels of unemployment were equal only to the excessive levels of police violence (Piven and Cloward 1979, 53–55). In 1934, Black residents in Harlem also led a rent strike after they found out that they paid almost twice as much in rent as the white residents who left the Sugar Hill building. The protests forced the local relief agencies to give residents money for rental payments and government officials to pass eviction moratoriums. For the most part, the rent strikes in New York were emblematic of a history of rent bargaining, where tenants formed short-term unions and hurled insults at landlords as a way to pressure landlords to stop evictions and fix up their buildings (Schwartz 1983). In New York City, the political response was twofold. One response was to pass protective stay of summary laws that legalized rent strikes. A resident of a tenement building was permitted to remain in their apartments during a rent strike as long as they made their rental payments to the court. The second response was to direct rent strikes and tenant organizers to public housing.

The federal government implemented social welfare housing policy solutions to address the affordable housing problem from the 1930s to the 1950s. Unlike Europe, public housing was and has never been a major part of America's affordable housing policy. Nationwide, the United States only built about 200,000 public housing units between 1949 and 1955. Almost all of the public housing was built in large cities. Public housing was part of the New Deal's Public Works Administration (PWA). Roosevelt created the PWA in 1933. He appointed Harold Ickes as the U.S. secretary of the Interior, a position Ickes held from 1933 to 1946, to lead the national program to build public housing. The federal government replaced the PWA with the U.S. Housing Authority in 1937, which then funded state-level housing agencies. Even though the PWA did not mandate that public housing had to be segregated, local authorities and policy makers segregated public housing projects. Seventeen of the 47 housing projects built were built for African Americans (Rothstein 2017, 20). The 1949 National Housing Act provided money to build public housing. However, local housing authorities still privileged working-class white applicants, built separate and segregated housing projects, and internally segregated the new high-rise housing projects. The notorious high-rise Pruitt-Igoe towers in St. Louis were segregated. Pruitt was for Black residents and Igoe was for whites. Although the Truman administration urged local housing agencies to build more public housing to address the housing needs of Black families in 1952, it came at the heels of the affordable housing shortage for whites.

Congress replaced the federal-controlled PWA with a system of local Public Housing Authorities in 1937. A new federal agency, the U.S. Housing Authority, authorized funding to local housing agencies, which had the power to make decisions over where to construct public housing. The public housing system was similar to the administration of the three pillars of the 1935 Social Security Act, in that degree of racial discrimination increased as it shifted from the federally run Old-Age Insurance program to the state-run Unemployment Insurance to the local level for means-tested programs (Lieberman 1998). The inclusion of excluded occupational categories in the 1954 and 1956 Social Security Expansion Acts is an example of how institutional changes to policy can create the conditions for Black men and women of all colors to obtain social rights. There was no such equivalent for the expansion of the right to mobility. Instead, the racial language of white-public created an affordable housing field designed to limit Black mobility even as public housing slowly opened to Black families.

Local control over public housing policy continued the practice of racially segregating public housing. The racial language of white-public achieved epistemic privilege in the affordable housing field. Its epistemic privilege created a symbiotic relationship between federal and local housing agencies. Indeed, Logan and Molotch (1990) rejected the notion that moving to a different level of government administration, specifically from the federal government down to local governments, meant that housing policy would achieve its social goals. They stressed the shared growth machine mindset that shifted federal funding to private development that had nothing to do with housing. However, the social goals of public housing were to provide housing to working whites. There were no broader social goals or housing or racial justice embedded in public housing. We can conclude that public housing was doing what it was designed to do: provide housing for whites and racially segregate the mid-twentieth-century metropolis. We can see this in the practice of the neighborhood composition rule and creating segregation where it didn't previously exist.

Local government officials institutionalized a neighborhood composition rule that mandated that public housing reflect the existing neighborhood demographics. The PWA defined the racial composition and thus racial classification prior to the construction of the housing projects. This illustrates how epistemic privilege creates cultural frameworks that guide how planners and housing agencies build the urban environment and housing. The official racial designation of a neighborhood was either a white or a Black neighborhood, and where there was ambiguity due to the reality of multiracial groups living in the same neighborhood, the neighborhood was defined as a white one. A neighborhood enjoyed many advantages if it was defined as white. One advantage was the absence of white political backlash. The political reality that federal PWA officials encountered was that even if the federal government wanted to construct interracial public housing, local white officials and prospective white tenants were against it. The New Dealers needed white support for their social programs and they could only secure their support by ensuring that New Deal social programs were racially segregated. Although civil rights activists like A. Phillip Randolph were able to pressure FDR into creating the Fair Employment Practice Committee to racially integrate federally funded worksites, racial integration at the workplace did not extend into the neighborhood.

Public housing created racial segregation in cities and neighborhoods that were not already segregated. They did this through land clearance. Local city governments combined zoning with the placement of public housing to consolidate racially mixed neighborhoods (Trounstine 2018). As Rothstein showed, "The government was not following preexisting racial patterns;

it was imposing segregation where it hadn't previously taken root" (2017, 14). Local officials demolished slums or tenements to make room for either public housing or some civic project or private development. The problem was that existing residents were displaced. In cities that had minimum income requirements to enter public housing, these residents were too poor to qualify for public housing. In cities like Chicago and Atlanta and St. Louis that reserved public housing for the very poor, displaced families, especially Black families, created overcrowded public housing projects. As municipal governments razed the slums in the name of progress and urban renewal, the local housing authorities used public housing to contain the inhabitants they displaced in the name of urban renewal. The concentration of Black individuals and families living in poverty is an example of Black immobility in a time of urban transformation. Local officials decided that in order for the city to renew itself, it had to carve out spaces and neighborhoods to contain Black and other racial minorities. Elite whites ceded city space to Black inhabitants but did not sacrifice their control over urban spaces or the city. The Black ghetto sits in a dialectical relationship with all forms of urban renewal and urban regeneration.

In addition to using public housing to segregate neighborhoods, housing agencies drafted lists to ensure that they only rewarded good whites with public housing. Working-class whites were the ideal type candidates because they needed housing and could make rental payments to defray the maintenance costs. The New York City Housing Authority (NYCHA) created a point system that allowed housing authority administrators to select not just white housing applicants, but good white families. Good white families created a positive image of public housing. The point system was modeled from the selection system used by private agencies to screen applicants for upper-class apartments (Bloom 2009, 70). The point system disqualified a family based on other classifications, such as a single-parent family household or having a criminal record, as well as subjective criteria such as a poorly behaved child. Applicants received additional points for a high family income and where they resided at the time of the application. Although this aspect of the point system was presented as objective, the existing forms of residential segregation per by block signaled to the administrator the applicant's race and social status. In turn, housing agencies used the selection system to ensure that 67% of public housing went to working-class whites.

The application system represented how public housing in theory was a universal right to shelter, but in practice was a practice that granted good whites the privilege of mobility. Working-class whites had the privilege not to live in the slums or tenements. It was a privilege that was formerly enjoyed only by the white middle and upper classes. The tenant selection system granted a diminutive right of mobility to middle-class Black families. That is, a narrow slice of good Black families could obtain public housing in majority-Black neighborhoods. In New York City, this created an intragroup hierarchy between Black families in Harlem who were able to get access to The Harlem River Houses public housing complex and Black families that did not meet the criteria. This hierarchy also existed in Chicago, but was spatially inverted because Chicago reserved public housing for the poor. In both cases, the selection of applicants followed the logic of segregation to divide public housing between white-public and Black-public housing. Whereas the NYCHA's selection system rooted in the language of white-public and good white citizenship granted whites the privilege of mobility, it only granted working Black families from a particular social class the diminutive right to housing in a segregated neighborhood.

The racial language of white-public created a field of affordable housing where state and market actors worked together to ensure that the public housing market did not threaten or undermine the private housing market. There was an obvious economic interest involved, as whites viewed the physical presence of Black inhabitants as devaluing their housing assets. Therefore, Black-public housing was limited to parts of the city that did not threaten white neighborhoods in the city or the suburbs. Cities also used federal funds designated for slum clearance to clear land and protect the private interests of banks, hospitals, and universities (Logan and Molotch 1990, 168). According to Freidland (1982), approximately 90% of slum and tenement housing units were destroyed and not replaced, and over 80% of the land went to private developers. The shift of public capital from public housing into the private real estate market was possible because it mirrored the federal government's objective of increasing the supply of market rate housing to drive economic growth.

The racial composition of public housing gradually changed from the mid-1940s into the early 1950s. The racial integration of public housing was the result of civil rights groups pressuring local elites. Similar to how elites in the 1930s responded to political pressure from the rent strikes, urban elites in over 200 cities responded to pressure from civil rights organizations, primarily from the National Association for the Advancement of Colored People (NAACP), to expand the number of public housing available to Black families (Hirsch 1983). In part, the integration of public housing was possible because the NAACP could prove racial discrimination existed in the public domain funded and operated by tax dollars. In the mid-1940s, the NAACP targeted public housing. In the early 1950s, they targeted school segregation based on the same logic. However, the opening up of public housing to Black families was made in relation to halting integration in the private housing market. The increased supply of homes through suburbanization pulled whites out of public housing. At first, local housing authorities left the public housing units vacant. Additional pressure from civil rights groups who wanted to fill these units with Black families and white homeowner associations that wanted to preserve their segregated white neighborhoods led municipal housing agencies to open additional housing to Black families. The continued pressure from civil rights groups to integrate public housing cumulated in 1962 when John F. Kennedy signed an executive order outlawing racial discrimination in public housing or urban renewal programs that accepted public funds.

The racial integration and demographic shift in public housing occupants from white to Black residents ended the field of white-public affordable housing policy. The reduction in the number of white families in public housing did two things. First, it shifted the working class and working poor whites out of public housing. This eliminated the mixed-class component to white-public housing that allowed local housing authorities to charge rent that offset the cost of maintenance. Ironically, the legal and cultural practices to maintain racial segregation actually kept Black-public housing as mixed class until the 1970s and 1980s (Wilson 1987). Second, it created the conditions for whites to enjoy the privilege of mobility. Combined with the elimination of racial zoning and racial covenant clauses, the integration of public housing universalized the right of mobility to all races. However, systemic white racism continued to prevent Black citizens from exercising this right. Regardless of their social class or financial means, Black citizen's immobility left them with limited choices of substandard housing and basically without a choice as to where they lived. Even the right to purchase property in the private market was limited. As I will document in the next chapter, the federal government's response to Black-public housing was to defund it while creating a portable and public subsidized white-private housing option that extended this privilege of mobility to poor whites.

RENT CONTROL AND THE RIGHT TO STAY

Rent regulations were the third aspect of white-public affordable housing policy. Rent regulations, either in the form of a hard cap that sets rents at a fixed rate or a soft cap that allows for annual increases tied to some external economic indicators, like cost of living, create the conditions for the right to stay. The right to stay is important when neighborhoods experience urban regeneration or gentrification, which accompanies increases in rents, and drives out existing residents. Rent regulations differ from public housing because it does not involve using public capital to build anything. As we will see in the next chapter, one critique of urban renewal was demolishing Black neighborhoods and forcibly removing Black families who did not want to leave. A formal right to mobility would have allowed them to stay or have a say in where they relocated to.

Federal rent control legislation was only possible because it was part of a larger white-public affordable housing field. Under a white-public political framework, the state used its monopoly of taxation and regulations to protect ordinary white citizens. In this case, it was protecting urban white citizens from the private rental market. If we view rent control in a longer historical context, there is not much of a history of the U.S. government using the power of the state to regulate capital like it did during the New Deal. Nor is there a history of the state using land regulations to grant citizens the right to stay in place. The U.S. government took lands from Indigenous peoples. The closest thing the United States did to guarantee the right to stay were the late nineteenth-century and early twentieth-century Homestead Acts that gave primarily whites the land the state took from Indigenous peoples (Feagin 2014, 55–57).

Rent control was even less of a national solution to the affordable housing crisis than public housing. The federal government passed wartime rent control as part of the Emergency Price Control Act (EPC) of 1942. The EPC placed price caps on a number of commodities that were deemed essential, including food and housing. In order to enforce the price controls on commodities and rents, the government created the Office of Price Administration. After the EPC expired in 1947, the federal government created the Federal Housing and Rent Act to enforce rent control regulations. Rent control targeted rent gouging in major cities. The mass migration of persons to major cities in search of jobs during the war increased the demand for housing. Major urban areas were already experiencing a housing shortage and mass migration pushed the housing supply to its limits, a ripe condition for rent gouging. As noted earlier, there was already a shortage of affordable housing because developers focused on the luxury housing market. These same developers were the most vocal critics of rent control. In spite of opposition, rent control was meant as a temporary price control on rents until the local housing supply could catch up with demand. And that's what happened. Federal rent control ended in 1950. But its story did not.

A select few states kept rent control and rent regulations on the books as an option, even if these regulations were suspended or only implemented in select cities. Two major U.S. cities under EPC rent control policy, New York City and Los Angeles, took different approaches to rent control after the expiration of the Housing and Rent Act. In order to understand why rent regulations continued in New York City but ended in Los Angeles, we have to understand how rent control operated to guarantee whites the privilege of mobility and in relation to public housing and the private housing fields in each city.

New York and Rent Control

New York State passed its own rent control laws in 1950. Although it applied to all cities in the state, including Buffalo, Rochester, and Albany, it was targeted at New York City. Approximately 2.5 million apartment units were regulated statewide, and 85% of all apartments in New York City were regulated (NYS Division of Housing and Community Renewal, 1993). While 22% of New York City's population was foreign born, 90% of the total population was classified as white in 1950 (U.S. Census, 1950). Construction of housing in New York City actually slowed down as capital shifted to the suburbs. The vacancy rate went from 16% in 1944 to 1% in 1955. There was still a housing shortage in the city.

New York State's rent control safeguarded the white privilege to stay without sacrificing the white privilege to relocate. Rent control was different from means-tested programs like public housing. Rent control is a form of universal affordable housing policy that grants whites of all social classes who rented the right to stay. In practice, this benefited whites who were already in the private rental markets. New York's rent control laws worked with the private and public housing market to supply affordable housing. Rent control was never an actual threat to the private housing market. It was not a threat because New York's rent regulations had limits. These limits did not impede the supply side of new housing construction. Only apartments built before 1947 were rent regulated. Single-family residences did not fall under the rent control laws. The reduction of new housing units in New York was due to capital moving to exurban and suburban regions. Land was cheaper. New single-family housing and apartment buildings were built in the suburbs of New York, like Westchester, whose population exceeded 600,000 in 1950. Thus, white families had options to move, and the subsequent suburban housing developments after 1950 increased their options (Gottdiener 1977). More importantly, the land was not controlled by old New York real estate families who held on to their properties like a miser and his pennies.

Los Angeles and Rent Control

In contrast to New York, California phased out rent control after the EPC Act expired. Even though Los Angeles endured a 20% population increase during the war, whites still comprised 93% of its population in 1950 (U.S. Census, 1950). Approximately 10,000 African Americans migrated to Los Angeles during World War II (Sides 2003). Similar to New York City, the population of Los Angeles was almost exclusively white. Los Angeles' Black population was contained in Bronzeville, a neighborhood formerly known as little Tokyo, which emptied due to the U.S.-Japanese internment camps

(Katz, Chesney, and King 2018). The existence of racial covenant laws out-lawed racial integration into white sections, thereby preserving white-public housing and rental units. Because of existing racial covenant laws and other means of enforcing residential segregation, including violence and the threat of economic sanctions, Black inhabitants were confined to racially segregated neighborhoods in the city. The Los Angeles City Housing Authority did not desegregate public housing until 1947 after whites began moving to Los Angeles' surrounding suburbs. Los Angeles city officials declared an end to the housing shortage, and thus, decontrolled all rental units in 1950.

During the war, rent control gave whites the right to remain in place in the central city as population growth surpassed the pace of new housing construction. But that did not last long. Los Angeles was the epicenter of wartime and postwar urban growth in California. There was also a new round of federal investment through military bases and engineering schools to attract good whites to California. Compared to New York City, there was an abundance of cheap land. Los Angeles and Orange County entered a housing boom after the war (Doti 2016). Single-family homes would define the urban landscape of Southern California. Whites benefited from the housing boom: the homes, the construction jobs, and the federally insured home financing to purchase the homes. This was different in New York, as new construction was either in suburban New York, such as Westchester or Long Island, or located in another state, like Connecticut or New Jersey. In other words, for a brief moment in time, California could increase the supply of affordable housing without relying on either public housing or rent control. The irony is that advantage turned out to be California's biggest weakness, as housing emerged as perhaps the number one urban problem in California by the mid-1960s.

CONCLUSION

The language of white-public helps to explain why the United States adopted multiple and at times competing forms of affordable housing policy, as well as why early twentieth-century elites could not stop the construction of affordable housing units. Because whites were the primary and, in some places, the only beneficiaries of affordable housing, elite opposition could not quell ordinary white claims for housing. The reason why was that the language of white-public equated the public good with the good of whites. The use of the state to fund and deliver public provisions only lasted because the beneficiaries of affordable housing were white. Of course, the state ensured that other interests were taken into account. The real estate industry, developers, and builders all influenced the state's decision to use the private housing market as the solution to the affordable housing problem. Their impact is seen in how public housing and rent regulations were secondary and temporary solutions to the wartime housing shortages. But without the language of white-public, it is hard to imagine that the state or local governments would have even pursued the limited investments in public housing that they did. This points out how American's equated whiteness to the public good when it came to housing policy.

The language of white-public created proximate fields between the public and private housing markets. This adds to the history of affordable housing by emphasizing the relations between different housing fields rather than overemphasizing or glamorizing either the role of the state or the role of the market in making housing affordable. Funding public housing and regulating rents in the public housing market can keep rental and housing prices affordable because it provides a market for excess demand to find housing until an adequate supply of housing can be constructed. Likewise, increasing the supply of housing that is affordable takes pressure off of the public sector because it makes homeownership for those who want it a reality. The case of the New Deal and postwar affordable housing policy illustrates that this did work at one time and can work today. Unfortunately, a combination of racism and the current neoliberal project prevents America from thinking in terms of using public capital to solve its housing problem.

Although the formation of a white-public affordable housing field was implemented to address the short-term problem of housing shortages for whites, it has had significant and enduring long-term effects on America's class and racial structure. The most glaring example is the relationship between wealth and homeownership between Black and white families that continued into the twenty-first century. The combination of state subsidies and racism in the real estate industry made ownership available to middle- and upper-class whites. When assessing the way that racism operates at an institutional level, scholars have a tendency to overlook how Black families make decisions to opt out of or never applied to available affordable housing programs. There was no point in applying for a mortgage if the banks were going to deny you the loan. There was no point in trying to purchase a suburban home if racial covenant prohibited the developer and homeowner from selling you the home. Having access to affordable housing through subsidized rents or public housing may provide shelter, but it does build wealth for the poor or working classes. Thus, the privilege of mobility works with economic rights. In this case, the privilege of mobility grants one access to the private housing market. The wealth gap anchored in housing continued as the state built generous tax advantages into the tax code. This includes the mortgage deduction. The mortgage deduction favors the wealthy and upper-middle class who pay a higher property tax based on the amount of the mortgage plus local property tax rates, which tend to be high in wealthy areas in order to keep out the poor. The long-term effects of the white-public era of affordable housing policy were creating a generational wealth gap between whites and between white and Black citizens.

NOTE

1. Racial zoning was still used in some Southern cities, including Birmingham, Alabama, until 1950 and West Palm Beach, Florida, until 1960 (see Rothstein 2017, 46–48). Federal laws don't mean much if they are not enforced. This was the case with school desegregation after the 1954 *Brown v. Board of Education* decision. Southern states did not actually begin integrating its public schools until 1970, after suburbanization and northern style racial segregation within southern urban areas became the norm (see Hohle 2015, 149–190).

Chapter 4

The Undoing

Affordable Housing in the Neoliberal Era

The white response to the growing Black population in America's cities led to the undoing of the New Deal era affordable housing policy. Approximately 33% of America's entire Black population migrated to cities after World War II. By 1960, 73% of the Black population lived in urban areas. Residential segregation in America peaked in 1970, the same year that the percentage of Black Americans living in cities reached 80%. A large number of Black families began migrating from rural areas to cities starting in the 1940s, a trend that accelerated in the 1950s and 1960s. Cotton began its structural decline in the 1930s. By 1967, the United States produced its smallest cotton crop since 1871 (Sweeney 1968). The introduction of the mechanical cotton picker in the 1950s ended the demand for Black agricultural labor in the Deep South (Beckert 2014). Black farmers migrated to cities where there were jobs at factories, at office buildings, at schools, and at the homes of elite whites. There was also the Black civil rights movement. From 1954 until the late 1960s, the civil rights movement led an ongoing struggle to racially integrate public spaces and institutions and neighborhoods. The white response was more than just a rejection of racial integration and African Americans securing claims to protective rights. Elite whites tore down the federal affordable housing system they built and shifted the responsibility of providing affordable housing to the private housing market.

The undoing of America's brief experiment with affordable housing was caused by the rise of a new racial language of white-private/Black-public. The racial language of white-private/Black-public originally emerged as a regional southern language in the segregationists and liberal business communities during the civil rights era (Hohle 2012). These two elite white groups were trying to reconcile how to maintain economic and political control over private and public capital as schools, institutions, and to a lesser extent, neighborhoods became racially integrated. The language of white-private/Black-public was slowly nationalized in the late 1960s and 1970s, ultimately providing the pretext for the neoliberal project. The shift to a language of white-private/Black-public created a new approach to affordable housing around subsidizing and socializing risk in the white-private housing market: the shift in capital investment from the city to the surrounding suburban housing market, privatizing public housing, and deregulating rent control. The common thread between these three responses was reinsuring the white privilege of mobility.

The American housing question differed between whites and racial minorities. The affordable housing problem for whites was rooted in maintaining the privilege to live in segregated white neighborhoods. The affordable housing problem for African Americans was getting actual access to the private and public housing markets. Existing Black neighborhoods were quickly becoming overcrowded and unsafe due to the high concentration of poverty found in racially segregated neighborhoods (Massey and Denton 1993). Black families paid more for housing and had a much harder time securing mortgages than whites did. The Black civil rights movement emerged as the biggest threat to whites' privilege of mobility. Ironically, the threat was not ending whites' right to mobility. Whites still had the option to live in whatever community that they preferred and could afford. The threat was that the civil rights movement would make the right to mobility available for persons of all races. The threat was ending whites' privilege to monopolize public capital and live in racially segregated communities. This meant opening up the private and the public housing markets to Black families. It was a demand for universal and equal rights.

Table 4.1 depicts how the language of white-private/Black-public created two parallel and racialized affordable housing fields. A white-private affordable housing field increased the supply of single-family market rate homes in the suburban areas. The state made public capital and tax subsidies available to developers, builders, and white families. On the one hand, capital investment simply moved to the suburbs. The *Milliken v. Bradley* decision, which stated that racial integration stopped at municipal lines, meaning that city school districts could not bus Black students to the white suburbs, fed the demand for suburban housing among white families. On the other hand, the type of capital investment in city centers remade central business districts. Local developers and city leaders used federal funding to reorganize central business districts around Finance, Insurance, and Real Estate; convention centers; and sporting venues. The new revitalized central business districts were connected to the suburbs by the interstate highway system. Furthermore, capital investment in the housing market was concentrated in

Table 4.1　U.S. Affordable Housing Policy and Race by Field, 1951–1999

Time Period	Context	Racial Language	Affordable Housing Policy	
			Public Field	Private Field
The Civil Rights Era				
1951–1979	1. Black migration to central city 2. Racial desegregation 3. Capital investment shifted to suburbs 4. Inflation and Stagflation 5. Deindustrialization	White-Private/ Black-Public	<u>White-Private</u> • 1965 Rent Supplement Program • 1968 Housing Act (Section 235 Rental Vouchers) • 1973–1980 HUD Experimental Housing Allowance Program • 1974 Housing and Community Development Act (Rental Certificate Program) • Rent Stabilization (New York) <u>Black-Public</u> • 1968 Fair Housing Act	<u>White-Private</u> • Urban Renewal • Model Cities • 1968 Housing Act
Neoliberal Era				
1980–1992	1. Banking Deregulations 2. Continuation of Deindustrialization 3. Shift from Rust Belt to the Sunbelt 4. Start home construction on periphery (outer burbs, edge cities) 5. Savings and Loan Scandal	White-Private/ Black-Public	<u>White-Private</u> • 1986 Low-Income Housing Tax Credit • Rent Stabilization (California) <u>Black-Public</u> • 1976–1998 Gautreaux program	
1993–1999	1. Consolidation of technology and finance into major metropolitan areas 2. Banking Deregulations 3. Racial integration *and* segregation of suburbs	White-Private/ Black-Public	<u>White-Private</u> • 1998 Quality Housing and Work Responsibility Act (Section 8 housing vouchers) <u>Black-Public</u> • 1999 Fairclough Amendment	<u>White-Private</u> HOPE IV (Empowerment Zones, Enterprise Zones, Choice Neighborhoods)

the Sunbelt, away from the concentrations of unions and Black residents in the city centers located in the Northeast and Rust Belt cities (Gottdiener 1994). The supply side market solutions still worked to provide affordable housing for whites.

A separate Black-public affordable housing field emerged during the 1960s. Whites rejected public housing once the social problems of poverty, unemployment, and police brutality that triggered the race riots of the 1960s were associated with public housing and the Black ghetto (Quadagno 1994; Gilens 1999). After negative racial meanings associated with Black marked public housing, white policy makers and public officials began the process to defund and privatize it. Public housing was privatized through the introduction of demand side rental assistance programs, specifically housing certificates and the housing voucher. Vouchers and certificates could be used in the private housing market. This granted poor whites the opportunity to live in the suburbs or majority-white city neighborhoods. Even if Black families could obtain a voucher in the 1970s and 1980s, they were still subject to racial discrimination in the private rental market. Public housing was defunded throughout the course of the 1980s and 1990s. This left poor and working-class Black families to the mercy of the bottom rung segment of the affordable housing market that is propped up by the housing voucher system. Whereas tax subsidies and Federal Housing Association (FHA) insurance socialized risk in the white-private housing market, and rent control placed a price cap on rents, the voucher system created an artificial and inflated rental floor in the Black-private affordable housing market.

New York and California's approach to rent regulations illustrates the centrality of white mobility at this time. The privilege of mobility means having the option to live where you want, including one's existing neighborhood. Theoretically, rent regulations should be the antithesis of the private housing market. However, we find how racism makes a market-oriented and a price control policy actually work together. A city's private housing market benefits from rent regulations because they allow whites to stay in transitioning urban areas and provide rental certainty for landlords with properties in economically distressed neighborhoods. Capital disinvests in neighborhoods that become predominantly Black neighborhoods. The demographics of a neighborhood matter. Rent regulations grant whites with a high degree of cultural capital the right to remain in urban neighborhoods. Not all members of the creative class are high-income workers, so their added cultural value to neighborhoods is found in their status as white artists, which has historically been a pull factor for attracting high-income workers to urban areas (Florida 2002). Racial languages make strange bedfellows out of otherwise contrasting forms of affordable housing policy.

CITIZENSHIP, HOUSING, AND THE
CIVIL RIGHTS MOVEMENT

The Black civil rights movement of the mid-twentieth century was by far the most significant social movement in the history of the United States. But it did not end racial inequality. Not even close. It did deracialize American citizenship and redrew the boundaries between who and what counts as good American citizens. The rewriting of citizenship removed enough legal and institutional barriers to begin the slow process of racial integration, which triggered a white response that changed American political economy. This included housing. Although the civil rights movement is primarily known for desegregating public schools and public spaces, and securing additional protective rights for Black citizens via the 1964 Civil Rights Act and the 1965 Voting Rights Act, the movement also made an important impact on housing. Urban social movements form in relation to their demands for collective consumption, which include access to resources such as water, electricity, education, and housing. Given that the civil rights movement involved collective consumption demands for housing, including access to water, schools, and even paved roads in many parts of the rural South, we can conclude that the movement was partially an urban social movement.

The Black civil rights movement created two distinct visions of Black citizenship. Each vision of citizenship was defined by assumptions on how best to proceed with racial equality. Each ideal type of citizenship included a set of practices on how to organize the Black community, how to interact with whites, and created normative ideals of the Black self. The first vision of Black citizenship was good Black citizenship. It was part of the movement's liberal project that emphasized racial equality through individual rights. Good Black citizenship emphasized projecting a racially nonthreatening self to secure individual citizenship rights as the means to achieve equality (Hohle 2009, 2013). Although scholars have discussed the role of nonviolence and direct action in the civil rights movement as the key to securing rights (see McAdam 1996), it was the emphasis on being racially nonthreatening that made nonviolence effective. After all, Black social movements were nonviolent prior to the civil rights movement and have remained nonviolent after the civil rights movement. What was unique about good Black citizenship was how it sought to deracialize Black political representation. What I mean by deracializing is that the movement sought to remove the existing negative stereotypes and negative meanings associated with Blackness while remaking an empowered Black political identity. The movement sought to use good Black citizens as a means to open up the private affordable housing market to prospective Black homebuyers. However, unlike the struggle for economic and voting rights, the struggle for housing rights did not turn out as they planned.

The civil rights movement fought against racial segregation prior to the Montgomery Bus Boycott and King's leadership. The National Association for the Advancement of Colored People worked with a handful of other organizations to form the National Committee against Housing Discrimination in 1950 to challenge laws on racially segregated low-income and market rate housing (Meyer 2000, 139). Members of CORE were particularly active in New York. They ran a demonstration called "Operation Window Shopping" where Black families toured legally segregated suburban housing developments (Meier and Rudwick 1975, 185). CORE also helped organize a series of rent strikes in Harlem. In 1963 the Lower Harlem Tenants Council challenged the eviction of Black tenants by withholding the rent (Schwartz 1983; Jackson 2006). The tenants demanded heat, electricity, and plumbing—basic amenities that should have already been provided by New York City law. Yet, the residents found that white city officials could be both sympathetic and shrewd. The New York City mayor created housing courts, sent building inspectors to enforce building codes, and fined landlords for not maintaining their buildings. City officials used the bureaucratic process of filling out forms and the court system to neutralize protests and side with landlords.

The liberal projects shifted their attention to urban social problems after the 1965 Voting Rights Act. The urban problems of note included the concentration of poverty, police brutality, and access to safe and affordable housing in Black neighborhoods. The shift from demanding national citizenship rights to securing urban citizenship rights thrust the liberal project into the complex world of landlords and city government. In 1966, SCLC went to Chicago to raise awareness about the squalid living conditions found in Black neighborhoods, the noncompliance of open housing ordinances that real estate agents used to prevent neighborhood desegregation, and landlords who refused to invest in the upkeep of their units, and support for additional federal housing (Garrow 1986, 501–507; Ralph 1993, 48). The housing problem in Chicago was a complex relationship between Black neighborhoods, Black aldermen, Black landlords, and Chicago's infamous Richard Daly's political machine. Martin Luther King Jr. moved his family into an apartment in the North Lawndale section of Chicago. Coretta Scott King described the building as dirty and smelling of urine. Because of the building's poor condition, King and other members, who called themselves the Chicago Movement, took trusteeship of the building. They dressed in work clothes, grabbed shovels and brooms, and cleaned the building. They used a mild rent strike until the landlord agreed to fix the building. Ralph (1993) noted that these attempts failed because the slumlord was an 80-year-old man who did not conform to an idea of a greedy and overzealous slumlord, and that King did not grasp that many of the ghetto slumlords were also Black. This also angered Black landlords because bringing their building into compliance with the city's building codes cost money. The Chicago Movement also organized the East Garfield Park Union to End Slums. They organized a meeting with two white landlords who owned over 30 buildings. The landlords shifted blame onto the banks and mortgage lenders who would not lend money to structures in the redlined Black neighborhoods. The result was the "Condor and Costalis Agreement" that established a series of obligations between landlord and tenant (see Ralph 1993, 64). Landlords were required to perform prompt and routine maintenance on the buildings while residents were required to follow specific rules governing tenant behavior. The emphasis on tenant behavior echoed the public housing tenant applicant codes from the 1930s and individualized the racist structures.

The limit of the liberal project was that it could not address Black citizens' right to mobility. The federal enforcement of economic and political rights could not break through the racial barriers erected by the state and white-private housing market. Although holding rent strikes and negotiating agreements with landlords and the city could theoretically provide marginal improvements to everyday material conditions, they inadvertently pinned Black individuals and families to segregated neighborhoods. As I will explain later, this pattern of demanding a right to public housing rather than a right to mobility inadvertently tied the Black struggle for housing to the Black-public housing field. In the end, the federal government's 1968 Housing Act was an homage to King's legacy, but the absence of any regulations to enforce open housing ordinances meant that mobility did not become a substantive right of Black citizenship.

The second vision of Black citizenship was Black authenticity associated with Black nationalism. Black authenticity refers to the embodiment of an idealized racially pure Black political agent (Hohle 2013, 2020). Black nationalist groups used Black authenticity as a cultural framework to create new institutions that were designed to address the needs of the Black community. This meant creating a Black-owned labor market, electing Black politicians to represent Black people, and rebuilding Black communities from the ground up. These competing visions of Black citizenship reflected the social and spatial positioning of the different groups. The roots of Black nationalism date back to the 1930s (Erdman 1938), as urban Black residents looked to carve out a Black first political identity (see Lincoln 1961). The resurgence of Black nationalism in the 1960s reflected the growing interest in Black authenticity as a means to redefine urban Black citizenship.

The Atlanta Project represents an example of how a Black authenticity organized the demand for affordable housing. In contrast to the liberal project emphasis on housing rights, the Atlanta Project addressed Black mobility. In Atlanta, it was the right to stay. Atlanta used federal urban renewal money to demolish Black neighborhoods (Pendergrast 2017). Although the existing slum conditions of Black neighborhoods were less than ideal, the Atlanta Project focused on improving the neighborhood rather than displacing Black families to another segregated Black neighborhood. The Atlanta Project targeted white slumlords on Markham Street in the Vine City neighborhood. The Atlanta slumlords carved up houses and rented each housing unit by the room. The Atlanta Project connected the slumlord to Atlanta's broader racist political economy, noting how one slumlord "established a plantation-like system in which he acts as landlord, employer, grocer, creditor, sheriff, judge and jury over the people who live on his property. He cashes their welfare checks, controls their credit" (Mende Samstein Papers, "Some Proposals for a Housing Campaign"). The Atlanta Project held a rent strike and constructed a tent city for Black families that were evicted for supporting the protests. These protest practices were claims for space. Making a claim for space is an exercise of power. A successful claim for a space like neighborhood is part of what affirms a group's identity. A claim for space is different from a claim for access to space. Access to space implies sharing space. The liberal project made claims for access to space because they wanted to integrate spaces, including, but not limited to, public housing and public spaces. Despite the efforts of the Atlanta Project, the city of Atlanta continued to bulldoze Black neighborhoods and reneged on promises to build either public or affordable housing, while its white homeowners turned their back to funding public initiatives or services that benefited Black people (Kruse 2005; Hohle 2015, 120–126).

A second example of Black nationalists addressing the housing question comes from the Black Panther Party. Huey Newton and Bobby Seal formed the Black Panther Party in 1966. The initial problem the Black Panthers targeted was police brutality, hence their original name of the Black Panther Party for Self-Defense. The question of housing appears twice in the Black Panthers' Ten-Point Program. It is number 4 "We want decent housing, fit for shelter of human beings" and number 10 "We want land, bread, housing, education, clothing, justice and peace" (Austin and Howard 2006). However, the Panthers' shift into housing came in the 1970s, after the party created their Programs of Survival (Hillard 2008). The Programs of Survival represented the Black Panther Party's shift from self-defense and cop watch programs to building new institutions around Black authenticity with a radical Black social consciousness (Hohle 2020). This shift to building new institutions paradoxically meant working within the context of Lyndon Johnson's Great Society programs. Some of the Black Panther's notable programs were the People's Free Medical Clinic (Nelson 2011) and the Free Breakfast for

School Children (Lateef and Androff 2017). Regarding affordable housing, the program of note was the People's Cooperative Housing Program. The People's Cooperative Housing Program focused on working with the federal government to build affordable housing for low-income Black individuals and families in Oakland (see Hillard 2008, 54–55). As was the case in many American cities starting in the 1950s, the elite white response in Oakland was to demolish Black neighborhoods in the name of progress and urban renewal. The Oakland Citizens' Committee for Urban Renewal (OCCUR), a group of local real estate elites, in this case white bankers, developers, and retail store owners, created the Oakland Redevelopment Agency (ORA). The ORA demolished the Black neighborhood in West Oakland, and left it vacant and undeveloped until the 1960s (Rhomberg 2004, 121). Whereas the private housing market increased the supply of housing for whites, the elimination of housing in West Oakland, combined with residential segregation, reduced the supply of housing for Black residents at a time of increased demand. Unfortunately, the Black Panthers did not have the capital to construct their own housing. It costs a lot more to enter the real estate market than it does to raise money for food or to find volunteers to run clinics. Thus, the Panthers used a clause in the 1949 Housing Act that stipulated any form of urban renewal that used federal funds to demolish housing must replace that housing if the citywide vacancy rate was 5% or less. Although the city of Oakland spent two years trying to stop the program, the Panthers' efforts found some success via the City Center Replacement Housing Program in Oakland.

The decline of the civil rights movement did not mean the end of Black struggles for affordable housing. Both the liberal project and Black nationalists targeted the white-private housing field and sought access to the same state subsidies readily available to white homebuyers and developers. Neither the liberal project nor the Black nationalists were able to make significant inroads in securing Black citizens' right to mobility in the white-private housing market. Middle- and upper-class Black families navigated through racist institutional barriers in the private housing market, especially the suburbs. This left Black urban social movements little choice but to concentrate their efforts on securing housing in the public housing field. For example, in the 1970s, the Welfare Mother's Movement, a social movement composed mainly of Black women, organized to change AFDC regulations pertaining to the suitable home statute that existed in some states (Hertz 1981). Black urban social movements claimed that public housing was a right and denying Black families housing violated Black civil rights. Even though the right to mobility includes access to private housing, the state's interest in protecting the rights of Black citizens in the white-private housing market did not match their interest in subsidizing the white-private housing market. The paradox was that the struggles for affordable housing through social welfare programs inadvertently reinforced the association of public housing with urban Black residents.

WHITE-PRIVATE SPACES: DISINVESTMENT, FLIGHT, AND RESETTLEMENT

The white response to the civil rights movement was a combination of austerity, privatization, and institutionalizing a regulatory field to protect white's racial and economic interests. The logic behind the white response was to create a new form of political and economic control that preserved white power and institutionalized white privilege. This included institutionalizing the privilege of mobility in lieu of the decline of de jure forms of segregation.

The federal government's primary approach to providing affordable housing was to continue the subsidization and regulatory scaffolding of the white-private suburban housing market. Although whites' economic and political interests were directly tied to real estate, their privilege to exercise power and access capital was directly tied to their race. While the economic gains and political power differed between elite and ordinary whites, all-whites had an interest in the production and maintenance of the white-private housing market. Suburbanization would have occurred even if Black America did not migrate to cities. American cities still had a problem of low vacancy rates and substandard housing that made the single-family suburban on a large plot of land in a quiet neighborhood home seem like paradise. However, the allocation and concentration of resources that established wealthy white places and Black ghettos and middle-class bungalows was the result of racism.

The logic of mid- to late twentieth-century housing policy was establishing a variety of white-private spaces. White-private spaces were racially segregated and private spaces, such as neighborhoods, shopping centers, and the location of jobs. One result of the establishment of white-private spaces was that it facilitated the formation of multicentered metropolitan regions (MCMRs) that began in the 1930s. The MCMRs are the contemporary spatial arrangements that are composed of multiple commercial hubs and residential settlement spaces that geographically extend across municipal boundaries (Gottdiener 1985; Gottdiener, Hohle, and King 2019). Rather than view urban areas as a dichotomy between the city and the suburb, the MCMR views urban settlement spaces as relational spaces. White-private spaces were created in relation to Black-public spaces. Whereas white-private spaces institutionalized white mobility, Black-public spaces institutionalized Black immobility. Black migration from rural areas to the suburbs represented a diminutive right to mobility historically exercised by migrant labor. I will discuss the relationship between Black immobility and Black-public housing in the next section. For now, I want to focus on the establishment of white-private spaces.

Two interconnected urban policy changes created white-private spaces. The first was the spatial reallocation of capital. The spatial reallocation of capital was the shift in public and private capital investment from city centers to suburban areas. The reallocation of capital accompanied austerity measures through the decline of federal money for urban areas and the select investments in commercial activities in city centers. The second was through the combined processes of privatization and deregulation that established multiple suburban housing markets through the logic of filtering. These processes were concretized through the formation of public-private entities to lead development schemes, homeowner associations, gated communities, and zoning ordinances around the single-family residences.

The Spatial Reallocation of Capital

The most significant shift in mid-twentieth-century urban development was the reallocation of capital from city centers to suburban regions. It was the one thread that connected Lydon Johnson's Great Society programs with the nationalization of the neoliberal era associated with Carter and Reagan. Although Great Society urban policy did not have the neoliberal stamp of austerity through reduced funding, it did apply austerity as a moral approach to budget making. As a moral approach to budget making, austerity involves allocating limited funds to one group at the expense of another group. We can see how the cutting and allocating of federal money created white-private and Black-public housing through the relationship between residential segregation and slum clearance during the period of urban renewal. The amount of federal money allocated for central city slum clearance and renewal increased in the 1960s, from $706 million in 1960 to $3.8 billion in 1970 (Mollenkopf 1975). Local elites targeted already existing Black neighborhoods for demolition. To do this, local elites rezoned entire Black neighborhoods from residential to commercial. Once rezoned, local officials could use federal money, including money from the 1956 Federal Highway Act, to demolish housing structures and create open spaces. Planners and developers rebuilt the city centers on these newly created open spaces and around service sector employment, like finance, insurance, leisure, and hospitality. They used modern highways to connect the city employment centers with the suburban housing markets. White federal officials offered Black families empty promises of replacement housing. In reality, Black families were relocated to other Black neighborhoods, anchored by Black-public housing projects, which created the problem of overcrowding and transformed slums into ghettos. Indeed, the percentage of Black persons displaced due to urban renewal programs exceeded 75% (Roberson and Judd 1989, 3). It was against this backdrop that James Baldwin uttered the phrase "Negro removal" in a 1963 television interview to capture the real intent of America's urban renewal efforts.

The Federal Model Cities Project is an example of how the language of white-private shaped Johnson's federal affordable housing policy. The Model Cities Project, which ran from 1966 until 1974, was designed to provide affordable housing and redevelop blighted neighborhoods. Unlike prior supply side approaches to increase the number of new housing units through municipal housing authorities, Model Cities included a provision to include local stakeholders. Local stakeholders included residents as well as the conservative trifecta of real estate elites, politicians, and business leaders. The latter had more input in the planning and administration of the program. Despite promising new affordable housing, Model City funding was used for administrative costs, to demolish buildings and clear land for private development, and moved existing Black families to public housing away from the development sites (Hohle 2013, 125–126). Poor and working-class white families protested against the proposed demolition and relocation, in part because they lived in white neighborhoods that were not overcrowded and not composed of dilapidated structures, and in turn, were less likely to have their neighborhoods razed. Only a fraction of the proposed affordable housing units was ever built. What the Model Cities program illustrates is how the local conservative elites used white-private to rationalize the reallocation of capital investment into the city center for the purposes of transforming the growing Black-public city centers into white-private commercial spaces.

The difference between the 1968 Housing Act and the 1968 Fair Housing Act captures how the federal government sought to secure whites' privilege of mobility in relation to Black immobility. The Fair Housing Act amended Title VIII of the 1968 Civil Rights Act to protect Black and other racial minorities from discrimination in the housing market. It technically outlawed redlining and blockbusting, even though banks informally continued those practices. In contrast, the 1968 Housing Act was a continuation of supply side approaches to increase the number of affordable housing units. The combination of these two housing acts institutionalized a white-private/Black-public approach to providing affordable housing. This racial distinction would all but take the ordinary white stakeholders out of the field of public housing and then place them squarely in the field of the private housing market. The privilege of white mobility for whites of all class and status distinctions was tied to the same fate.

The 1968 Housing Act was designed to address the problem of affordable housing for whites. Although the number of housing starts averaged about 1.4 million a year in the 1960s, it was not enough to meet the demand for suburban housing. The Department of Housing and Urban Development (HUD), whose origins lay in the House and Home Finance Agency until Johnson established a cabinet-level position to oversee housing policy, was responsible for managing the 1968 Housing Act. HUD officials used a color-blind language to define public housing as a program that was too slow to act and that HUD could not produce housing fast enough (Von Hoffman 2012). The only option left to the state was to help increase the amount of affordable housing in the private market. Von Hoffman (2012) explained how the state adopted the big business approach to increasing the housing supply. The Johnson administration formed a commission made up of leading actors in the private home construction industry. It was known as the Kaiser Committee. The committee's work led to Section 235 and Section 236 of the 1968 Housing Act. These sections lowered interest rates and expanded the use of the FHA insurance to low-income buyers, made the federally subsidized credit market available to nonprofits to build housing, and offered rental subsidies (figure 4.1).

In the 1970s, the total number of completed new housing units decreased after 1973. The year 1973 was the year of the oil embargo that triggered massive price increases and inflation. However, the drop in total housing units was driven by the reduction in the number of buildings with five or more housing units. These are the types of structures built as rental units. The construction of single-family homes dropped in 1973 but had recovered by 1976. The recovery in the single-family market combined with the decline in multiunit housing structures indicates how capital investment shifted to the suburbs at a time that the need for housing increased in the city.

The 1968 Fair Housing and Housing Acts institutionalized a white-private housing market and a Black-public housing market. Following the logic of white-private/Black-public, the Nixon and Reagan administrations cut money that supported Black-public housing and social welfare. The Reagan administration also cut money to address urban poverty in poor cities and HUD funding. I will discuss the changes to public housing in the next section. For now, the question is what happened to the white-private affordable housing market? The answer is found in how the old racial language of white-public was marginalized as a regional and local policy, and thus, so was the Keynesian project. The series of deregulations in the banking and housing industries in the 1980s focused on the luxury suburban housing market. A new lexicon to capture the white-private spaces where new housing construction took place emerged in the 1980s: the outer suburbs, edge cities, gated communities, and gentrification. The common

denominator was that this white-private housing market was a luxury housing market for upper-class and wealthy whites.

Regan's vision of a neoliberal affordable housing is captured in the lengthy
1982 "The Report on the President's Housing Commission" published by
HUD. The report summarized Reagan's approach to affordable housing:

> President Reagan's Commission on Housing approached its task with optimism
> based on an entirely different belief: that the genius of the market economy,
> freed of the distortions forced by government housing policies and regulations
> that swung erratically from loving to hostile, can provide for housing far better
> than Federal programs. (xvii)

The commission used the language of white-private to rationalize the privatization of affordable housing. The report stated that affordable housing was
a supply problem that negatively affected primarily whites and the real estate
industry. The report noted that those affected by an affordable housing shortage were young couples, empty nesters, young professionals relocating to the
city, thrift institutions, and home builders. The closest thing to addressing the
needs of the poor or Black inhabitants was to note that low-income families
were spending a high proportion of their income on adequate housing. Rather
than a right to housing and shelter, the report redefined the American housing
question as a problem of affordability that could be answered by the private
market.

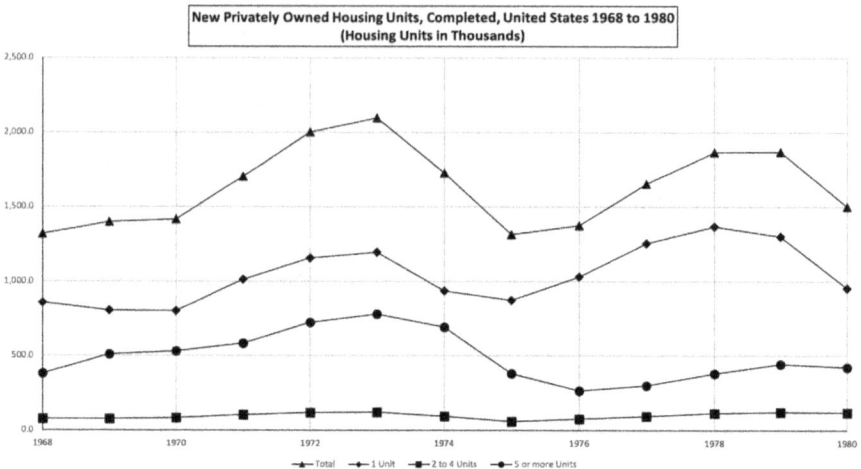

Figure 4.1 New Privately Owned Housing Units, Completed, United States,
1968–1980.

Reagan's housing commission contained a generic seven-point program that would define the neoliberal approach to affordable housing policy:

1. Achieve fiscal responsibility and monetary stability in the economy
2. Encourage free and deregulated housing markets
3. Rely on the private sector
4. Promote an enlightened federalism with minimal government intervention
5. Recognize a continuing role of government to address the housing needs of the poor
6. Direct programs toward people rather than toward structures
7. Assure maximum freedom of housing choice.

These seven points guided how the Reagan administration approached housing. The idea of shifting the responsibility to the private market to provide affordable housing echoed his 1982 Private Sector Survey on Cost Control, also known as the Grace Commission, that urged privatization of government services where a profit could be made. The discourse of affordability shifts the responsibility of affordable housing from the state to the individuals and families. It recasts affordability as a series of good and bad choices on what one spends their money on. It adds a moral component to housing that did not exist prior to the neoliberal turn. Good citizens make good and responsible housing choices, where personal responsibility is realized through living within one's economic means. Of course, the rising costs of housing are not tied to individuals or families choosing to live in an expensive house when cheaper options are available. Reality and negative impacts never got in Reagan's way when it came to policy.

Reagan's perfunctory approach to affordable housing was the Low-Income Housing Tax Credit (LIHTC). The LIHTC was part of Reagan's signature 1986 tax reform, a tax reform act that lowered the top marginal tax rate while also taxing unemployment benefits for the first time. The logic of the LIHTC was to grant tax subsidies to private developers to offset the cost of building low-income housing. In part, the privatization of affordable housing of LIHTC has to be understood in relation to the austerity measures placed on public housing. Reagan placed a moratorium on project-based subsidies like public housing in 1981 (Williams 2004). Money allocated for public housing decreased from over $30 million in 1980 to less than $10 million in 1987, resulting in 120,000 fewer new HUD-subsidized housing units in 1985 than what was built in 1980 (Stearns 1988, 206). This left affordable housing up to local policy makers and developers. The result was that approximately 75% of construction that received LIHTC subsidies were complexes in already racially segregated and deteriorated neighborhoods, many of which were multiunit apartment complexes (Rothstein 2017, 190). The LIHTC subsided real estate elites while reinforcing existing forms of racial and class segregation.

Another housing problem emerged at the end of the George Herbert Bush Administration. The academic and policy debates over the nature and role of the urban underclass and residential segregation made policy makers aware of the negative effects caused by residential segregation. In 1989, Congress formed a commission to study the problem of distressed housing and the deteriorating condition of public housing. The Bush administration handed off the problem to the incoming William Jefferson Clinton Administration. The result was the HOPE VI program. The HOPE VI program was the first comprehensive example of neoliberal urban policy (Hyra 2012). Consistent with the federal housing programs in the 1960s and 1970s, HOPE VI used public funds to demolish existing affordable housing units, in this case public housing, to make way for new private market affordable housing, and relocate the poor. HOPE VI had two notable policy components: Empowerment Zones and Enterprise Zones. Once HUD officials classified an area as highly distressed, they extended tax credits and subsidies to developers and businesses operating within the area to redevelop and rehabilitate the structures. The state's goal was to remake blighted areas into mixed use areas that combined residential and businesses. HUD policy makers borrowed the concept of mixed use, which was originally made popular by the urban critic Jane Jacobs in *The Life and Death of Great American Cities*. Whereas Jacobs used the term "mixed use" to champion diverse and mixed-class neighborhoods, HUD wrapped the language of white-private around mixed use to redefine it as a diversity of commercial and residential real estate interest. Subsequent research on the HOPE VI projects found no substantial improvements for existing residents or residents in nearby neighborhoods (Oakley and Tsao 2007; Oakley et al. 2015).

What the HOPE VI project did was reboot the logic of urban renewal of the 1960s and 1970s that equated creating white-private spaces with urban development. Similar to the era of urban renewal, local politicians used a discourse of opportunity that was embedded in the Enterprise and Empowerment Zone policies to relocate Blacks families to new neighborhoods. The discourse of opportunity advanced an assumption that all the social ills attributed to the Black ghetto would be cured via the spatial deconcentration of poverty. In turn, the discourse of opportunity masked the role of white racism. In practice, Blacks families had the right to housing located at the periphery of the city-suburb boundary or the inner ring suburbs. It followed the logic of filter down housing: Black families had access to housing only after capital created new and more exclusive white-private spaces.

Thus, from the 1950s to the end of the twentieth century, the language of white-private provided the rationale and logic behind using the private housing market as an affordable housing policy. The underlying logic was creating the conditions for whites to exercise their right to mobility. The increase in the housing supply was for whites. The difference from the start of this era to the end of this era was how the federal government slowly moved toward subsidizing the luxury suburban housing market and redeveloping city centers. In turn, this created the conditions for the rise of two distinct settlement spaces in late twentieth-century urbanization: Black suburbanization and gentrification.

Filter Down Housing and Suburban Developments

Suburbanization as a form of affordable housing is dependent on federal tax subsidies that make the single-family home affordable. The single-family home connected ordinary white families with the real estate sector and land use policy. The real estate and construction industry was a $100 billion industry in the 1970s, about nine times the size of the automobile industry (Gottdiener 1995, 242). Suburban political and economic elites formed land development corporations to purchase land on the basis that it would be used for residential and commercial development. Suburban commercial development meant creating structures for professional occupations and building retail centers, such as plazas and shopping malls. These amenities paired with homeownership to create a self-sustaining and segregated ecosystem of family-work-leisure. The regional composition of multiple economic centers meant creating an urban political economy where whites neither lived nor worked in the Black-public city. There was no reason for whites to return to the city center. Building the suburbs around the single-family home made sure that white families had a direct economic stake in the white-private housing field. This network institutionalized the preferences of white homeowners and shaped residential mobility and settlement spaces throughout the twentieth century (Trounstine 2018). White homeowner's main preference was keeping the suburbs segregated.

The logic of filtering down combined with zoning regulations to tie the white-private affordable housing and luxury housing markets together. Zoning ordinances bound white homeowners', developers', and local governments' political interests. The initial wave of zoning ordinances was designed to prevent Black families from relocating to the suburbs. This was originally accomplished through the use of racial covenants and redlining, as I noted in the previous chapter. The "spirit of racial zoning" (Hohle 2018, 141) guided the practice of a second wave of zoning ordinances that occurred in the 1970s.

The demand for suburban housing continued to increase after a series of federal court decisions, notably the 1970 *Alexander v. Holmes*, which mandated that schools actually be desegregated and 1974 *Milliken v. Bradley*, which placed spatial limits on which schools had to be racially integrated. Suburban developers and governments used up zoning or exclusionary zoning to create more exclusive and expensive suburban housing. Exclusionary zoning meant increasing the square footage of single-family homes and the size of the lot to reduce density even more than what the original low-density zoning accomplished. Existing suburban homeowners could choose to sell their existing home and upgrade to a new larger and more expensive home. Following the market logic of filtering down, older suburban homes became available to more working- and middle-class white families. The white-private market succeeded in building its way out of the problem of a potential shortage of homes in white-private spaces.

Ensuring that Black Americans have the same right to mobility as whites do means addressing the dual problems of racism and class inequality in the private housing market. In part, all prospective homeowners faced the problem of affordable housing. When we adjust for inflation, the median cost of single-family homes increased 43% in the 1970s (U.S. Census Historical Census of Housing Tables, 2000). Adjusting for inflation, the median income increased 4% for whites and 2% for Blacks and Hispanics from 1970 to 1980. The rising cost of housing beyond income was the main grievance of white Californian homeowners who backed Proposition 13 in 1978. The housing market of the 1980s followed the economic boom-and-bust period that bookend the decade, as housing starts declined after the Volcker Shock and double dip recession of 1981 to 1982 and then again after the savings and loan scandal and market crash of 1987 (Ball 1994). There were also key geographical differences in the cost of housing due to the rise of and concentration of the finance and technology industries in large metropolitan regions. For example, nationally, the median increase in housing prices in the 1980s was 4.3%. In New York City it was about 64%. Prospective Black homeowners in the 1970s and 1980s faced an additional problem of racism that continued to restrict and limit Black migration from the city centers to suburbs and a federal government that was not interested in building or subsidizing housing for Black families.

Black suburbanization was the result of housing in the aging inner-ring suburbs filtering down to Black families. Clay noted that even the initial post-1970 wave of Black migration to the suburbs represented "more of a resegregation of Blacks in particular sectors of suburbia than dispersal in an open housing market" (1979, 405). The demographic shift in suburban living occurred in the 1980s and 1990s. In large metropolitan areas, 37% of the Black population lived in the·suburbs in 1990, a number that increased to 44% in 2000, and then to 54% in 2010 (Frey 2001, 2011). We have to understand that the filtering down of suburban housing to Black families was relational to new white-private settlement spaces. The process of Black suburbanization occurred as whites were constructing white-private spaces in the outer suburbs, edge towns, gated communities, and gentrifying city centers. In contrast, Black suburban areas were more likely to face problems of poverty, an aging infrastructure, crime, lower property values relative to white suburbs, and tend to be located adjacent to Black neighborhoods in the city center (Gottdiener 1977; Schneider and Logan 1982; Pattillo-McCoy 1999). The combination of racism and the filtering down of housing created a mirage of Black mobility. Similar to the earlier era of Black migration to cities, Black residential options in the 1980s and 1990s were conditioned on financially well-to-do whites relocating to more exclusive white-private spaces.

WHITE-PRIVATE VOUCHERS AND BLACK-PUBLIC HOUSING

The combination of Black migration to cities and the civil rights struggles to secure affordable housing changed the cultural meanings associated with public housing. Gone was the notion of using public housing in conjunction with the private market. Public housing worked with the private market because both were largely restricted to white working families. When public housing worked with the private housing market in metropolitan areas, it was able to increase the supply of affordable housing while reducing the number of families living in the slums. The relationship between the public and private housing fields ended once public housing became defined as Black-public and populated with exclusively poor families. This triggered two significant changes in public housing policy. The first was privatization that reinsured the privilege of mobility for poor whites. The second was austerity that further limited poor Black individuals and families the right to obtain shelter. The result was that poor Black claims for affordable housing were channeled into public housing while poor white claims for affordable housing were situated in the white-private public housing market.

The two most significant developments in affordable housing policy came via the 1968 Housing Act and the 1974 Housing and Community Development Act (HCDA). Both acts exemplified how the language of white-private/Black-public created separate affordable housing fields for white and Black families. The introduction of housing vouchers and rental certificates guaranteed the privilege of mobility for whites by opening a limited sector of the private housing market to poor whites. It also began the structural shift away from fixed public housing, and shifted the responsibility of supplying housing for the poor back to the private housing market. Related was the introduction of austerity measures to reduce funding for fixed public housing, which left Black families in need of housing assistance to the mercy of the segregated white-private housing market. The combination of privatization and austerity transformed the federal approach to housing from a supply side approach to build fixed public housing to a demand side approach designed to support the private housing market.

The White-Private Housing Voucher

The logic of the white-private voucher was tying the privilege of white mobility to the private housing market. Whereas the initial wave of segregated public housing gave whites the right not to live in slums, there was no policy that granted poor whites access to the postwar suburban housing market. The 1968 Housing Act introduced rent subsidies, which was the precursor of the private housing voucher. It was proposed as a solution to more efficiently provide affordable housing than building new fixed public housing units. The 1968 Housing Act was more complex than the introduction of rental assistance. The 1968 Act also called for additional money for public housing. HUD also increased the number of subsidized public housing units between 1969 and 1972. However, the introduction of vouchers symbolized the reintroduction of privatization into affordable housing policy. This included allowing Public Housing Authorities (PHAs) to purchase buildings directly from private developers and the introduction of direct rental subsidies. Section 235 of the 1968 Housing Act provided a public subsidy to families who qualified for public housing that could be used to secure housing in the private rental market. Real estate elites and liberal reformers previously suggested using some form of rental assistance or vouchers as an alternative to public housing. Liberal reformers, real estate elites, and conservative politicians teamed up in the 1930s, 1940s, and 1950s to oppose New Deal era public housing (Bloom 2009; Von Hoffman 2012). Their rationale was that direct rental subsidies protected poor families from private landlords raising rents, and that scattering poor families across urban space could deconcentrate poverty and solve urban problems. The 1965 Rent Supplement Program also allowed for direct rent subsidies but only in buildings developed and managed by nonprofits.

So, why the renewed interest in white mobility in 1968? For one, suburbanization was well into its fourth decade by the mid-1960s. The suburbs were aging and capital was already seeking cheaper land for subsequent upscale housing development on the outer suburbs. This loosened up the supply of housing in the inner ring suburbs and outer city areas, which allowed available housing units to filter down to the working class and the poor. The question was how to make sure that poor whites could access these areas. The combination of Black migration to urban areas and the system of segregation and policing that created the urban race riots of the 1960s pushed whites out of mixed race and predominantly white neighborhoods located next to predominantly Black neighborhoods.

The question of how to secure the privilege of mobility for whites continued into the 1970s. The federal enforcement of school desegregation only increased white demand for all-white or majority white neighborhoods in the 1970s. The problem was that poor whites who wanted to relocate to white neighborhoods could not afford to do so. Nixon era budget cuts meant that public housing was a diminishing option for whites, and the racialized meanings and deteriorating conditions of the existing public housing stock meant that there was no real white preference, among elites or poor whites, for public housing either. There was a series of important movements that eventually coalesced into the modern housing voucher captured in the Section 8 Housing Program authorized by the HCDA of 1987. One was HUD's Experimental Housing Allowance Program, which took place in 12 U.S. cities between 1973 and 1980, and gave rental assistance to about 18,000 families, to test the impact of housing vouchers and advance privatization of public housing (see Arias 2013). Another was the 1974 HCDA. HCDA introduced the Rental Certificate Program, an extension of Section 235 of the 1968 Housing Act, and created the Housing Choice Voucher Program via an amendment to Section 8 of the 1937 Housing Act. This dubbed the voucher programs Section 8, a moniker that has lasted into the twenty-first century. Rental certificates provided a monthly payment to a private landlord to make up the difference in the cost of rent and either 30% of the voucher holder's net income, 10% of their gross income, or a percentage of their means-tested benefits designated for housing (HUD 1995). The only restrictions were on rental units that exceeded an area's average rent, a restriction that HUD reserved the right to wave. In 1975, HUD passed new regulations that prohibited local rent control laws from applying to rental certificate vouchers (Keating 1983, 2). There were no major changes to rental certificates and Section 8 housing vouchers from 1987 to 1997. Then in 1998, HUD passed the Quality Housing and Work Responsibility Act (QHWRA) that converted what was left of the rental certificate program into housing vouchers. The major change in voucher policy was it required families to pay at least 30% of their adjusted income on rent. Rather than provide affordable housing, vouchers continued to reinforce residential segregation (Krzewinski 2001). The absence of any kind of price cap with a demand side voucher created the conditions for predatory landlord practices and a profitable system for landlords at the margins of the private housing market.

A Black-private housing market formed at the margins of the white-private housing market. The Black-private housing market was made up of voucher and non-voucher holders located in the inner cities abandoned by capital during the Reagan Administration. Maney and Crowley called these spaces a "Section 8 submarket" because the voucher holders could only rent in neighborhoods that matched their race (2000, 335). Landlords play a key role in creating and maintaining a Black-private housing market. As Rosen (2020) showed in her ethnography of a Baltimore neighborhood, landlords directed white renters who can pay their rent to properties located in white neighborhoods where the existing residents will accept them because of their race, and Black families with housing vouchers to predominantly Black neighborhoods where renters cannot always pay their rent. In other words, the voucher gives the landlord rental certainty in Black-private or Section 8 submarkets. Because white-private affordable housing is located in areas with access to better schools, poor white families with vouchers can at least access functioning schools and reside in more class-diverse neighborhoods. In theory, vouchers meant that poverty could be a temporary and undesirable part of the life course rather than a life sentence for whites in urban areas. For the poor of all races, the right to mobility protects one from the negative effects of capitalism in urban areas—the concentration of resources and persons into defined spaces. When only one racial group enjoys this right, that right becomes a privilege in the form of having a realistic chance of beating poverty.

What would a privilege of mobility look like if it were available to Black families? This was the case of the Gautreaux program. As the Gautreaux program showed, when Black families were granted the right of mobility, their life outcome also improved relative to the life outcomes of Black families who did not have access to vouchers. The Gautreaux program was the result of a 1976 Supreme Court decision *Hills v Gautreaux* that found that racially segregated public housing violated Section 5 of the 1964 Civil Rights Act. Rather than rehab or repair or construct new public housing units, HUD and the Chicago Housing Authority awarded 7,500 housing vouchers to Black families living in Gautreaux. Some families moved to the suburbs while other families chose to stay. The Gautreaux program created a natural sociological experiment. Those who moved out of the racially segregated and high poverty neighborhoods found that their lives improved. In contrast to those that stayed, Black families who moved experienced better employment as adults, their children obtained a better education, and social integration between whites and Blacks increased (Rubinwitz and Rosenaum 2000). Rather than place a moratorium on housing policies and practices that maintained racial and class segregation, Gautreaux validated the voucher. The vouchers gave good Black families a chance more so than extending a universal right of mobility to all Black families. By limiting Black mobility to a narrow slice of

Black families, the voucher program did not threaten the white-private housing market. Whites have always tolerated some racial integration so long as it did not usurp their control over political and economic resources.

In sum, the language of white-private prevented the voucher program from having real success as an affordable housing policy. Although a narrow slice of good Black families was able to relocate to the suburbs in the 1980s and 1990s, residential segregation never went away for Black families of any social class. In some respects, poor whites with vouchers had more options on where they could live than middle-class Black families did. Vouchers disproportionately benefited whites who desired to remain in urban areas, but could not afford suburban homes, and did not want to live in racially mixed or Black neighborhoods. As the federal government lifted restrictions on where one could use a voucher, suburban housing also became an option for whites. The white-private voucher was first and foremost a policy to guarantee the privilege of white mobility.

Austerity and Black-Public Housing

By the mid-1990s the demographics of public housing residents versus those receiving vouchers reflected the dual white-private and Black-public affordable housing circuits. According to a 1995 HUD report titled "Public Housing: Image versus Facts," there were approximately 3,400 PHAs managing 1.3 million public units in the United States. More importantly was who lived in public housing compared with who received a voucher. 40% of public housing residents were over 65 years of age while another 43% of public housing residents were families with children, of which 56% were single parents. In part, public housing became senior housing. However, 48% of public housing residents were Black compared with 19% of voucher holders. Whites made up 39% of public housing residents but were 66% of voucher holders. There were 1.3 million families who received a housing voucher in 1995, with another 660,000 applicants on a waiting list (Krzewinski 2001). This demographic snapshot indicates the cumulation of 30 years of the restructuring of affordable housing policy in the white-private/Black-public era. One is that white-private voucher system protected poor whites' privilege of mobility. The other is that the Black-public housing market was defunded and reorganized to house qualifying seniors.

The federal government defunded public housing once it became defined as Black-public housing. The relational nature of Black-public and white-private created a cultural framework that understood public housing and vouchers as incompatible. Going back to the mid-1960s, one of the reasons why there was such an influx in the number Black families in public housing had to do with the reallocation of the capital into the white-private suburbs.

Urban renewal funds were routinely used to demolish housing units and land clearance in Black neighborhoods. However, in 1965 the federal government passed a new law. The 1965 HUD Act stated that any persons or families that were forced to relocate because of urban renewal funds having to do with the Highway Act had the right to public housing. In other words, we have to understand the racialization of public housing in relation to the realloca-tion of capital via urban renewal and suburbanization. Federal and municipal governments relocated Black families to a single neighborhood anchored by a racially segregated public housing complex, but only after whites had left the city center and entire metropolitan regions were being reorganized around white-private settlement spaces.

The Nixon Administration froze all new public funds and expenditures to public housing in 1973. The freeze lasted for 18 months. Elites and other government officials looked at the state of public housing and declared that it was a failure. They blamed the style of architecture, the deteriorating physical conditions of the buildings, and the concentration of poverty in and around housing projects. What they did not blame was the cause: the racist austerity measures imposed on local PHAs. Indeed, Bloom (2009) rejected the notion that the architectural form of high rights building created all the problems surrounding public housing. Using the example of New York City, which has the highest number of public housing units in the country and has high-rise apartments, Bloom argued that what separates NYMHA from other PHAs is that New York has a history of managing large properties. On top of that, the problems associated with public housing did not exist when they were adequately funded. The decline of the federal government's support for public housing came after public housing became almost over-whelmingly occupied by Black families. The same high-rise construction projects did not have the problems or negative reputations when they were racially segregated and there was a mixture of white working-class and poor families.

For all intents and purposes, the public housing experiment in America ended during the Clinton Administration. The main neoliberal housing proj-ects of the 1990s, specifically the HOPE VI program and the Fairclough Amendment, which was part of the QHWRA, were policy extensions from the previous decades of privatizing public housing. This program and that amendment reflected the overall neoliberal reforms to social welfare that shifted the responsibility of caring for the poor and providing affordable housing to the for-profit and non-for-profit private sectors. The HOPE VI program provided public funds to local municipalities so that they could demolish severely distressed public housing. Over 150,000 public hous-ing units were demolished between 1997 and 2007. HOPE VI also granted PHAs the power to evict and relocate families from distressed public housing units if they refused to leave voluntarily. The 1999 Fairclough Amendment capped the number of public housing units that Americans could ever build to the number of housing units that existed in 1999. There were 1.41 million public housing units in 1994. HUD is limited to replacing units on a one-for-one basis. The federal government cannot increase the supply of public housing without amending or abolishing the Fairclough Amendment. The only national affordable housing policies left are the demand side vouchers and tax subsidies for the white-private housing market. By 1999, American citizens in need of housing reached an all-time high of 5.3 million, while the average wait to receive a voucher, if voucher lists were not already closed, was 28 months (Maney and Crowley 2000). The wait time for a voucher in America's three largest metropolitan regions was 10 years in Los Angeles, 8 years in New York, and 5 years in Chicago.

DEREGULATING RENT REGULATIONS: FROM RENT CONTROL TO RENT STABILIZATION

Two types of affordable housing problems emerged in California and New York in the 1970s. The financialization of the economy, the rise of the technology sector, and the globalization of the American media and entertainment sector were the most significant economic factors remaking America's urban regions. The common thread between these economic forces was that they concentrated specific types of capital and people in select coastal cities in New York and California: finance in New York and technology and entertainment in California. Yet, the restructuring of the urban economies had different effects on population growth in both states. The story of California is a straightforward narrative of population increases outstripping the supply of housing. California's population increased 123%, over 13 million new residents, from 1950 to 1980. Much of California's urban population growth was centered in Los Angeles. The population of Los Angeles County increased 80%, or roughly 3.3 million new residents. In comparison, the population of New York stagnated between 1950 and 1970, only to decrease by 10%, or by about 823,000 residents, from 1970 to 1980. Although New York State still enjoyed an 18% population increase between 1950 and 1980, New York's economy was undergoing a massive economic restructuring as it transitioned from an industrial to a postindustrial economy. The problem of affordable housing, then, was driven by who rather than how many people were migrating to major urban centers. White professionals began returning to the cities that endured 20 years of capital disinvestment. They increased the demand for housing that was in short supply. Subsequently, housing prices began to rise and existing white residents were threatened with displacement. It was a problem that could not be solved with filter down housing, suburbanization, housing vouchers, or public housing. In California and New York, the solution was the deregulation of rent regulations to create more available housing for professional whites and the conditions for ordinary whites to remain in the city.

The affordable housing problem that emerged for professional whites in the 1970s triggered a crisis in white mobility because the mobility options for one set of whites were relational to another set of whites. Whites struggled to purchase homes in white areas or remaining in their current homes due to rising rents. They needed an affordable housing policy that protected their privilege to obtain housing and remain in place. This was different from Black struggles for affordable housing at this time. For one, Black movements struggled for access to a limited supply of public and substandard private housing in neighborhoods around public housing projects. The language of Black-public combined with residential segregation to curtail Black's right to mobility. Second, there was no federal policy to regulate the private housing market. This shifted the responsibility to the states to provide affordable housing. Real estate interests have a lot of power and influence at the municipal and state level. They made sure that any state or local affordable housing policy protected the interests of real estate elites and landlords. The result was rent stabilization. As we will see, rent stabilization ensured whites had the privilege to remain in gentrifying neighborhoods and protected landlord interests in the private rental markets.

The First Wave of Gentrification

Gentrification was the second distinct form of settlement space of the late twentieth century. Gentrification refers to the socioeconomic and sociocultural restructuring of urban space, typically a neighborhood. There are three interrelated dimensions to gentrification. The first is the supply side, which includes the role of government and the movement of capital investment to distressed neighborhoods (Smith 1996). The second is the demand side, found in the establishment of new amenities that make the area attractive to outsiders, specifically white professional and upper-class residents. The third dimension is displacement, meaning the persons and families who were living in the gentrified neighborhood were forced to leave because they could no longer afford to live there or they no longer felt like they belonged there. Gentrification was one of the reasons that housing costs rose in the late 1970s and early 1980s. Not all whites exercised their option to move to the suburbs. The historic city centers still had majority-white neighborhoods. Other whites, seduced by images of the bohemian city, wanted to return. The nationalization of the neoliberal project through a series of tax reforms, banking, and housing deregulations created the conditions for white-private capital and whites to return to the city. This created a new form of settlement space known as gentrification.

The first wave of gentrification in the 1980s and 1990s did not lead to the end of the Black ghetto nor did it create affordable housing. What it did was create exclusive spaces for wealthy and upper-class whites who had a nuanced relationship with the existing residents.[1] The real estate sector played an important role selling young white professionals—or yuppies—on the image of gritty neighborhoods filled with excitement and lots of upside (Mele 2000). In other words, the same network of white homeowners, real estate elites, and government actors that produced white-private spaces in the suburbs produced the new gentrified white-private spaces in the city. The key difference is that gentrification required displacement in order to carve out white-private spaces whereas suburban development relied on building communities on vacant land. The key similarity is that Black, Hispanic, and poor families of all races were excluded from both.

New York and Rent Regulations

When the majority of American's think of rent control, they think of New York City. And for good reason. They were the one major U.S. city that continued with the rent control experiment after the EPC Act expired in 1947. New York's response to the demographic shifts in New York City was to deregulate rent control. In 1962, the state of New York transferred control of the rent control program to the city. Although they shared administrative responsibilities, New York City had the authority to alter laws. In 1961, 85% of all apartments in New York City were under rent control, even though the number of rent-controlled units decreased from 2.5 million in 1950 to 1.8 million in 1961 (NYS Division of Housing and Community Renewal 1993). Similar to the public housing regulations of the 1937 U.S. Housing Authority Act, new rent regulations included subjective interpretations of the number of children in the family relative to the size of the apartment. The logic of these regulations was to exclude undesirable renters, especially Black renters. The city allowed for luxury apartments to exist outside of the rent control regulations. Due to a political backlash from ordinary whites who experienced an affordable housing crisis caused by a low vacancy rate of 1.23% in 1968, down from 8.8% in 1965, and rising rents due the disappearance of rent-controlled apartments, the city introduced rent stabilization in 1969.

In contrast to hard price caps set by rent control laws, rent stabilization allowed for automatic yearly increases. New York City created new agencies, the Rent Guidelines Board and the Rent Stabilization Association, to develop and administer a set of rent regulations pertaining to the landlord-tenant rental exchange. Within rent stabilization, a private contract between renter and landlord sets the basis and conditions for a tenant's right to stay in a unit. Regarding economic cost, the main regulation introduced was the Maximum Base Rent (MBR) formula that calculated the maximum amount a rent a landlord could charge. As long as the landlord did minimal upkeep on the building and avoided any serious building code violations, they were eligible to raise the maximum rent on the building. This allowed for variations in the amount of rent a landlord could charge, which depended on variables such as location and size of the apartment. Rent stabilization only applied to apartment buildings constructed between 1947 and 1969. However, rent control laws were still on the books, and applied to residents or their direct descendants who still resided in the wartime rent-controlled apartments. This was an institutional advantage for white tenants since Blacks and Hispanics were essentially excluded from renting in certain New York neighborhoods.

A second round of white-private deregulations occurred in 1971. The combination of high inflation and low vacancy drove up rents, prompting those with rent control or rent stabilization to stay where they were. In this sense, rent stabilization was working for renters, but not for landlords. In 1971, Governor John Rockefeller signed a vacancy decontrol ordinance into law. Vacancy decontrol allowed landlords to decontrol or destabilize any rental unit once the tenant vacated the unit. This meant that the rental unit was placed back onto the rental market at market rate prices. Approximately 300,000 rent control units were decontrolled, and 88,000 units were destabilized, which led to a 52% rent increase in decontrolled apartments and a 19% increase in rent for destabilized apartments (NYS Division of Housing and Community Renewal 1993). Whereas economists would predict the removal of rent control and stabilization would lead landlords to invest capital into their properties, the New York City Commission on Costs and the Economy found that increases in landlord profits led to a 30% decrease in renovations. This led to actual displacement and the threat of new displacements, which prompted local residents to pressure the city to insert new protective regulations into rent-controlled units. The result was the 1974 Emergency Tenant Protection Act (ETPA) that ended vacancy decontrol and placed units that were decontrolled back onto rent stabilization ordinances. However, similar to other rent control laws, the ETPA exempted units built after 1974 from rent stabilization. Even after the state resumed control of the administration of the rent stabilization program, the ETPA still provides the regulatory framework for rent stabilization in New York City today.

During a time of racial and economic transition in the five Boroughs, the ETPA rent stabilization program gave whites the opportunity to stay in desirable neighborhoods on the upper west side of Manhattan and Greenwich Village, while also allowing developers to construct new buildings in desirable areas. The preservation of white bohemian neighborhoods served as a cultural pull factor that brought white and young white-collar workers back to the city, especially to SoHo and the Lower East Side neighborhoods in the 1980s (Mele 2000; Zukin 2014). This was in sharp contrast to the distressed areas of New York, such as the South Bronx, where landlords abandoned an estimated 10,000 units a year (Grossman 1975) or burned down their buildings for the insurance money. Although rent stabilization was in effect across the entire city, it did not deter capital investment into real estate in the predominantly white neighborhoods. Thus, the city could address the problem of affordable housing for whites because rent stabilization provided options for whites to stay put, protected landlord profits in older buildings in a time of economic transition, and exempted new buildings from rent stabilization to attract new capital investment into real estate in the city (figure 4.2).

With the exception of New York's 1984 Omnibus Act that switched administrative control of the rent stabilization program back to the state, New York did not make any further deregulations to the rent stabilization policy. That changed in 1993. Under the leadership of a Republican governor and the Republican-led state senate, New York passed the 1993 Rent Reform Act. The 1993 Rent Reform Act deregulated the rent stabilization laws in favor of landlords and real estate developers. Landlords gained the ability to deregulate vacant apartments if the legal rent was $2000 a month. Although the original deregulation only pertained to apartments vacated in a specific time period, from July to October of that year, the state's renewal of the ETPA in 2003 made the law permanent. The white-private deregulations created the opportunity for landlords to invest in their properties for the purpose of destabilizing the units. It was similar to previous rent deregulations that removed barriers for capital investment into real estate while protecting white tenure. At this time, the classic NYC tenement landlord, the local landlord who were long-term building owners and knew how to navigate the rent-regulated field (Sternlieb 1966), was replaced by professional real estate investors with close ties to the finance industry, whose investment strategies are based on capitalizing on potential rents rather than investing in distressed urban areas (Teresa 2019).

As we can see in table 4.2, when we adjust for inflation, there were double-digit rent increases in every borough from 2000 to 2017. With the exception of Staten Island, the real value of rents continued to increase after the recession. As I will discuss in detail in the next chapter, the financialization and globalization of the U.S. housing markets linked the housing markets of places like New York City with global investment markets. However, we can't ignore the impact of the 1993 Rent Reform Act in creating the conditions for landlords to decontrol their apartments. In a time of increased real estate speculation and global investment into New York, New York needed the type of pre-1993 Act rent regulations. Rent regulations alone will not solve New York's affordable housing problem. More housing needs to be built and steps have to be taken to decommodify housing.

Rent Regulations in California

Select cities in California adopted rent regulations as an affordable housing policy. One major contextual difference between California and New York is that California had plenty of land to build new housing. New York City is landlocked. Yet, California's white homeowners and real estate interests negated this geographical advantage overtime. The preferred structure in New York is a multiunit apartment building or condominium. The preferred structure in California was then and is now the single-family home. The dominance of the single-family home created a subgroup of whites, the white homeowner, whose economic and political interests were tied to the real estate field. Thus, California emerged as a political arena for dueling urban social movements. White urban social movements focused on property taxes and rent regulations in the private housing market while Black urban social movements focused on access to public housing.

White homeowners emerged as a political force in the 1970s. They mobilized as white Not In My BackYard (NIMBY) movements in relation to issues of taxation and affordable housing. For example, consider the tax revolts. The California tax revolts were made possible by the convergence

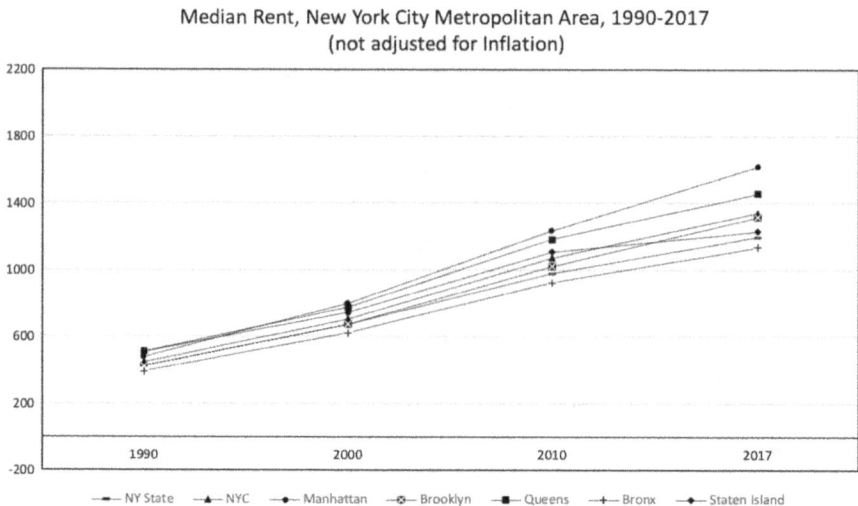

Figure 4.2   Median Rent, New York City Metropolitan Area, 1990–2017.

of white homeowners, business groups, and government officials. Although each had distinct interests, the common concern that brought them together was high inflation, the rise of property taxes, and the debate over the fairness of property assessments (Sears and Citren 1985; Purcell 1997; Martin 2008). Although the tax revolts originated in the white middle classes, upper-income white homeowners and the California Real Estate Association joined with them and helped pass Prop 13, which rolled back property taxes to their 1975–1976 value and capped annual property tax increases to 1% a year and assessments to 2% a year. However, landlords did not pass on the savings to renters. By 1979, 55% of all California residents rented their homes (Keating 1983, 2). Housing activists pushed back. They formed alliances with left-wing mayors and city councils. The result was rent control and rent stabilization.

Rent regulations differed city by city in California. Prior to the tax revolts, Berkeley, California passed local rent control laws in 1972. The legacy of the radical student movements of the 1960s created the context for housing movements to mobilize for rent control. In this regard, Berkeley differed from San Francisco, where the local tenant movement worked through the San Francisco Housing Authority to improve the quality of public housing, especially in San Francisco's Black neighborhoods of Hunter's Point, Porters Hill, and the Western Addition Projects (Barton 1985, 2011; Baranski 2007). The real estate industry pushed back against rent control. The California State Supreme Court ruled that Berkeley's municipal charter that made rent control a permanent law was ruled unconstitutional. However, Governor Jerry Brown vetoed a state legislative measure that would have given California the power to preempt local rent control laws (Keating 1983, 3). Without a state-managed rent control program, California's local municipalities had the authority to implement and manage their own rent control programs. This led not only to variation in rent regulations between cities, but also explains why some cities passed rent regulations and other cities did not. In Santa Cruz, for example, the local real estate elite's influence over local politics meant that city officials struck down any rent control or rent stabilization laws (Domhoff and Gendron 2009). Between 1977 and 1982, twenty-seven cities in California passed some form of rent control or rent stabilization policy. Berkeley and Santa Monica passed rent control laws, while the others passed rent stabilization policies. Los Angeles County approved rent stabilization in 1979, and made it a permanent policy in 1982. White residents in Beverly Hills and West Hollywood were the main beneficiaries of rent stabilization. Unlike rent control, Los Angeles' rent stabilization ensured landlord profits by permitting annual rental increases, and allowed for a unit to be decontrolled once it was vacated. In contrast to New York, there were no vacancy controls in Los Angeles, and Proposition 13 that froze

Table 4.2 Median Rent, New York City (Inflation Adjusted to 2010)

	2000	2010	2017	2000–2010	2000–2017	2010–2017
NY State	863	977	1065	13.21%	23.41%	9.01%
New York City	905	1,071	1,154	18.34%	27.46%	7.71%
Manhattan	1,022	1,234	1,390	20.76%	36.03%	12.64%
Brooklyn	863	1,021	1,131	18.36%	31.11%	10.77%
Queens	995	1,181	1,253	18.71%	25.95%	6.10%
Bronx	796	923	975	15.97%	22.50%	5.63%
Staten Island	953	1107	1058	16.22%	11.08%	-4.43%

Source: Citation, U.S. Census of Housing; American Community Survey 2013–2017, 2010 ASC 5 Year Estimates.

property taxes, combined with the availability of cheap land on the periphery of the Greater Los Angeles metropolitan region, meant that new housing units had to be constructed away from the city centers to ensure real estate profits and provide state revenue.

While California was implementing white-private rent stabilization, the state and private capital continued to disinvest in Black neighborhoods. There were no rent stabilization policies for Black neighborhoods because rents were not increasing. The problem of crime and blight stemming from previous disinvestment deterred future investment. As noted above, Black struggles for quality housing were confined to the public housing sector. In some areas of Los Angeles, Black activists and political leaders rejected rent control because they viewed it as an additional deterrent for potential capital investment (Katz, Chesney, and King 2018). Capital investment never arrived. Instead, Los Angeles used urban renewal funds to demolish the Bunker Hill and Chavez Ravine neighborhoods near downtown rather than build affordable housing (Davis 1990) (figure 4.3).

Unlike New York, California made major changes to its rent stabilization laws in the 1980s and 1990s. Due to pressures from landlords and real estate elites, who mobilized through the California Apartment Association (CAA) and the California Realtors Association (CRA), California passed the Ellis Act in 1985. The Ellis Act allowed landlords to evict tenants from a property and remove the building from the rental market if the landlord chose to leave the rental business. In practice, this permitted landlords to evict tenants and then sell the property to a new investor who was not required to

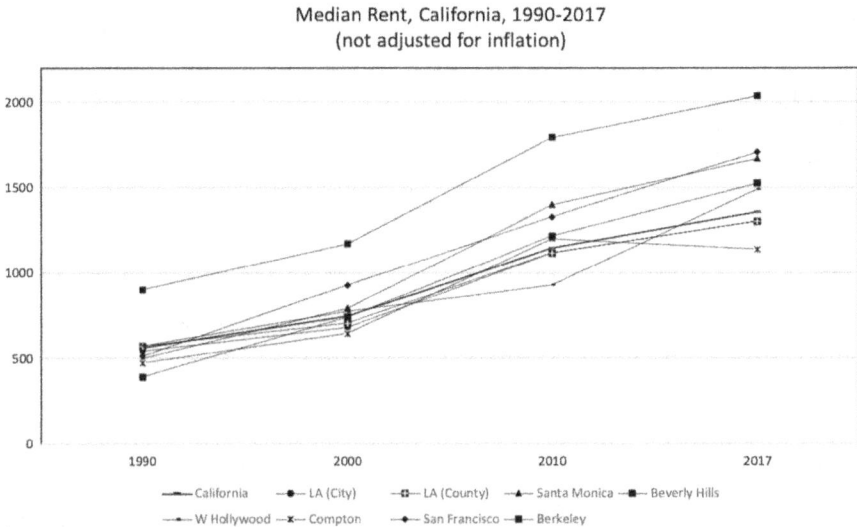

Figure 4.3   Median Rent, California, 1990–2017.

place the units back on rent stabilization. Then, in 1995, California passed The Costa-Hawkins Act. Costa-Hawkins exempted rent control or rent stabilization on apartments, single-family homes, or condominiums built after February 1, 1995. It also abolished statewide vacancy control, allowing landlords to increase rents to market levels when tenants vacated the property. In the context of federal stimulus from HOPE VI, the Ellis and Costa-Hawkins Acts provided an institutional framework for the construction of new market rate luxury apartments, as well as converting affordable housing units into luxury apartments and condominiums. While critics singled out NIMBY movements for blocking new housing developments, Costa-Hawkins led to the disappearance of affordable housing units from the rental markets.

There are two important points of data located in table 4.3. The first is that all parts of Los Angeles County and the Bay Area experienced double-digit increases in rent from 2000 to 2017. More importantly, the rental increases surpassed 40% in Berkeley and Santa Monica, the two cities that had the strongest rent regulations in the state, and two urban areas with notable tenant protection laws. This points to the dual effects of the Costa-Hawkins to decontrol units and California strict zoning laws that limit the type and amount of new housing construction. The other notable data point is that Compton—the historically Black and now majority Latino city in Los Angeles County—saw a 15.4% decrease in inflation-adjusted rent after the recession. As I will explain in more detail in the next chapter, this points to the predatory lending practices of banks and financial institutions regarding the increase of Black homeownership and Black-owned housing prices during the recession. In the absence of real estate speculation and bubbles, the fact that professional and high-income whites do not look for housing in majority-minority neighborhoods in an elastic or inelastic housing market indicates that we cannot ignore the importance of racism and the languages of racism in the American housing question.

CONCLUSION

The neoliberal era was the great undoing of the multifaceted approach to affordable housing established during the New Deal. This chapter showed how the emergence of a new racial language of white-private/Black-public contributed to its undoing. When the dominant racial language was white-public, federal and state responses to affordable housing provided multiple forms of affordable housing for white families. The white response to Black migration to urban areas and the civil rights movement's success in racially integrating public institutions triggered a new language of white-private to

Table 4.3 Median Rent, California (Inflation Adjusted to 2010)

	2000	2010	2017	2000–2010	2000–2017	2010–2017
State of California	959	1,147	1212	19.60%	26.38%	5.67%
Los Angeles (city)	874	1,117	1162	27.80%	32.95%	4.03%
Los Angeles (county)	904	1,117	1180	23.56%	30.53%	5.64%
Santa Monica (LA County)	1017	1,398	1489	37.46%	46.41%	6.51%
Beverly Hills (LA County)	1503	1,795	1817	19.43%	20.89%	1.23%
West Hollywood (LA County)	992	929	1330	-6.35%	34.07%	43.16%
Compton (LA County)	828	1,201	1016	45.05%	22.71%	-15.40
San Francisco	1191.27	1,328	1525	11.48%	28.01%	14.83%
Berkeley	950	1,217	1359	28.11%	43.05%	11.67%

Source: Citation, U.S. Census of Housing; American Community Survey 2013–2017, 2010 ASC 5 Year Estimates.

limit public and private resources for affordable housing to white families. The dominant approach was using tax credits and subsidies to increase the supply and subsidize the demand for white families to move to the suburbs. Much of the supply side approach to affordable housing relied on the logic of filter down housing. Filter down housing worked for white families. However, for Black families, filter down housing meant access to neighborhoods in the outer city and the aging inner-ring suburbs. It did not lead to the end of racial segregation. The state responded to demographic changes in public housing with austerity, in the form of cutting funding over maintaining structures, and a new white-private voucher system. The voucher system supports the margins of the private housing market while also making it possible for poor whites to live in predominantly white neighborhoods. Finally, the white response to urban decline and regeneration in California and New York City was to deregulate rent control. The use of rent stabilization allowed whites who already resided in the city and wanted to remain in their desirable neighborhoods the right to stay. Since rent stabilization allows for annual rental increases, it gives landlords both rent certainty and the option to take their buildings off of the rental market.

The shifts and modifications within the affordable housing policy fields maintained the white family's privilege of mobility. While it is apparent that suburbanization benefited whites by ensuring the white right to segregate, this same white privilege of mobility was embedded in the housing voucher and rent stabilization. Suburbanization, especially as it developed over the course of the twentieth century, also meant class segregation between whites: class distinctions between suburbs and city and then class distinctions between suburbs. Housing vouchers allowed poor whites to access housing in white neighborhoods. Vouchers allowed white families to raise their kids in segregated white neighborhoods. White neighborhoods accompany a different opportunity structure and are not subjected to the same levels of capital disinvestment or government austerity like Black neighborhoods are. Rent stabilization illustrated how white homeowners, landlords, and renters are all tied to the same white-private housing market. Rent stabilization created the conditions for whites to stay while also creating plenty of loopholes for real estate interests to make a profit. As we will see in the next chapter, white homeowners have become a very powerful political voting block against subsequent affordable housing.

Finally, looking at the neoliberal era through the lens of urban citizenship and the white privilege of mobility means we should think about the crisis of capitalism that hit cities in the 1970s as a racial-political crisis. The shift of capital investment to the suburbs indicates that capital investment in urban areas still occurred. It just didn't occur in places where Black people lived. What changed was how the language of white-private/Black-public recoded and separated the proximate housing fields that supported the public and private housing markets. The white response to the racial integration of urban areas transformed white-public spaces into white-private spaces. The success of the white-public Keynesian approach allowed whites to move out into other parts of the metropolitan regions, especially the suburbs. While interest rates increased in the 1970s, it did not stop the white-private housing market from expanding. Instead, what changed was how the Black-public housing field was no longer connected to the white-private housing field.

NOTE

1. There is a vast literature on the demand side aspect of gentrification that ranges from newly arrived whites directly and indirectly displacing existing poor whites or ethnic and racial minorities by introducing new amenities that cater in taste and cost wise to the gentrifiers. Yet, empirical research shows that some gentrifiers want to preserve some aspect of the old-timers culture because it creates the feeling of authenticity. For reference, see Brown-Saracino (2017) and Hyra (2017).

Chapter 5

America's Housing Question in the Twenty-First Century

America was courting a systemic affordable housing crisis throughout the 1980s and 1990s. Affordable housing has always been a problem for the poor and for racial and ethnic minorities. Marginalized urban citizens never have a choice in where they live. But ever since the 1930s, the state has generally protected whites from this housing malady. What was new about the start of the twenty-first century was how rapidly the problem of affordable housing expanded to whites, even the white middle class. There has been so much focus on the role of inequality in the neoliberal era and following the 2008 Great Recession, and justifiably so, that the housing question lurked in the background undetected, except by those on the margins. Interestingly, affordable housing became a larger problem after the recession and after elites saved the economy.

Table 5.1 depicts how the racial language of white-private has limited federal affordable housing policy since the turn of the twenty-first century. The language of white-private enjoys an almost hegemonic epistemic influence over affordable housing policy. On the one hand, the preceding developments in the affordable housing policy from the 1950s to the end of the 1990s privatized the field of affordable housing. The private housing voucher helped shady landlords much more than residents in need of safe and secure housing. The programs that were not privatized but subject to austerity, like fixed public housing units, or deregulated, like state-level rent deregulations that allowed for housing units to be decontrolled, led to a direct reduction of affordable housing options. On the other hand, the federal response to the early twenty-first-century housing question became limited to using market-based solutions to fix ongoing affordable housing crisis caused by neoliberal housing policy. The most important development was the financialization of housing. The financialization of housing is more than just the dominance

Table 5.1   U.S. Affordable Housing Policy and Race by Field, 2000–2020

Time Period	Context	Racial Language	Affordable Housing Policy	
			Public Field	*Private Field*
2000–2020	1. Financialization of housing	White-Private/ Black-Public		White-Private
	2. 2008 Great Recession			• 2008 Housing and Economic Recovery Act
	3. Black suburbanization			• 2010 Promise Neighborhoods

of financial actors in the field of affordable housing. It also involves the introduction of market practices, measurements, and narratives that end up rescaling and restructuring entire economies (Aalbers 2016). The language of white-private created the conditions for the financialization of housing starting in the 1980s. The reason why is that the financialization of housing needed pro-banking deregulations to reconfigure the housing market. Interestingly, the financialization of housing had unintended consequences on whites' privilege of mobility. By syncing local housing markets with global housing markets, the state could no longer ensure that whites could be insulated from spikes in housing prices or the systemic effects of the 2008 Recession. The paradox is that more whites endure the problem of affordable housing and segregation levels remained the same across the urban region. This caused white citizenship to splinter into two separate forms that sit in a tenuous alliance with one another.

This chapter is broken into three parts. The first part looks at the emergence of America's twenty-first-century housing question in relation to the fracturing of white-private citizenship that occurred in the very late 1990s and early 2000s. White citizenship fractured as an internal challenge from whites who felt as if their control over political and economic life, and the terms of good citizenship, was slipping. This created two competing forms of white citizenship. The first form was a continuation of the liberal form of white-private citizenship that stressed personal responsibility and economic success. This ideal of citizenship emphasized education and self-care practices as a means to overcome social problems without committing to structural changes. This form of white citizenship emphasized diversity without integration. The second ideal of white citizenship fused white-private citizenship with white ethnonationalism. This ideal used whiteness as a common destiny to tie whites of various ethnicities and social classes with an American national identity. The second part addresses the role of finance and globalization on housing markets. The financialization of housing linked local housing markets with global investment markets. Despite 40 years of neoliberal banking regulations, the bursting of housing bubbles, and the social damage done to neighborhoods, the housing question was largely ignored by whites because these problems were overwhelmingly located in Black neighborhoods and affected Black residents. That changed after private equity entered the housing market and builders cut back on production. Black families basically exchanged one type of affordable housing problem for another.

The last part of the chapter looks for hope. It looks for hope in how contemporary urban social movements have returned to the social problem of housing. After decades of the federal and state governments ignoring affordable housing, Yes In My BackYard (YIMBY) movements and Community Based Organizations (CBO) have filled the policy and idea void as they fight for an increased supply of and access to new housing. Is YIMBYism enough to answer the American housing question? Unfortunately, no. My critique is that they are inadvertently repeating the mistake of past housing social movements by conflating affordable housing with white mobility. The answer to America's housing question is a combination of granting Black and other racial and ethnic minorities the same right to mobility enjoyed by whites and through the creation of new public housing fields that remove speculation from housing.

FROM CRISIS TO RESPONSE TO THE RESPONSE TO THE CRISIS: THE ROLE OF RACE, FINANCE, AND GLOBALIZATION ON TWENTY-FIRST-CENTURY HOUSING

Real estate is like the overall business cycle in that it goes through periods of boom-and-bust. There are periods of overinvestment and speculation that inflate the value of real estate, creating a bubble that eventually bursts. Capital from the primary circuit of capitalism of production switches to the secondary circuit during down cycles. Although related and connected, their boom-and-bust cycles have not always been in sync. As noted in chapter 1, real estate and urban development are economic drivers in and of itself. They are not dependent on either industrial or postindustrial production. However, the early incarnation of the American neoliberal project in the 1980s brought these two circuits together through the financial sector. By syncing the two circuits of capital through finance, it created the conditions for a down cycle in either production or real estate to have systemic effects on the overall economy. As the neoliberal project expanded its global reach in the 1990s and 2000s, housing began to respond to a global housing market rather than local housing markets (Lees, Shin, and Lopez-Morales 2016; Madden and Marcuse 2016). Despite these universal political and economic changes, there have been uneven effects along the lines of geography, race, and social class. In other words, the crisis and response to the twenty-first-century housing question are rooted in citizenship.

As inequality between elite whites and everyone else grew, even between them and other whites, so did elite white power. Elite white power is embedded in the longer history of racial and class relations. Elites are able to deploy new racial languages to create connections between ordinary whites and themselves on the shared basis of whiteness. The last major shift in the racial languages occurred as a response to the civil rights movement. Evidence suggests that the language of white-private went through modification in the early twenty-first century. This modification of white-private split white citizenship into two competing ideal types: a liberal good white-private citizenship and a white ethnonational citizenship.

The first ideal type of white-private citizenship is the liberal form of good citizenship. Good liberal citizenship was a continuation of good white-private citizenship that defined whiteness in the neoliberal era. What was different is how it built off the foundational characteristics of personal responsibility and economic success and added ideals of individual self-improvement as a means to overcome social problems. This ranged from subjecting oneself or others to different pedagogies and therapies that would educate good whites out of racism, out of financial hardship, and out of bad relationships. It embraced diversity without forgoing any of the white privileges enjoyed by good whites. It did not change white's privilege of mobility. In theory, good whites actively seek out and champion small slices of diversity but do not welcome meaningful racial integration or create the conditions for Black and other racial minorities to have a meaningful degree of civic inclusion. Therefore, good liberal white citizenship maintains the privilege of mobility, to stay in gentrified areas where proximity to a limited number of Black or other racial minorities is an enhancement of their white cosmopolitanism, or to reside in predominantly white neighborhoods and support institutional reforms so long as these reforms do not infringe on white privilege.

The second form of white citizenship is ethnonationalism. It emerged from the increase in racial precarity among whites. In part, it revived dormant racial troupes and discourses of the nation and otherness embedded deep within the white racial frame. White ethnonationalist citizenship stressed a race first white identity. The rise of white ethnonationalism appeared on the margins of the neoliberal project. It was a reactionary movement of elite and upper-class whites who created political alliances with ordinary whites. This movement responded to new forms of racial integration, notably the increased number of Black people entering predominately white spaces, such as higher education (Chun and Feagin 2021) and suburban homeownership. Although the white-Black binary continued to anchor America's racial structure, Latino and Hispanic and Asian populations were becoming more visible in public discourse and in political circles, especially in the Sunbelt and on the west coast. The early 2000s' housing boom demanded labor. Developers and builders used migrants, some illegal, some from Mexico, willing to work off the books. Builders and developers hired workers off the books to avoid paying payroll taxes. Ordinary white and even Black workers balked at what they saw as illegals stealing "their" jobs. On September 11, 2001, America was the victim of a terrorist attack led by Arabs of Saudi descent. America responded by invading Iraq and Afghanistan in the name of preemptive war. In contrast to America's past international enemies during the cold war, the new international terrorist was othered *and* racialized. The discourse of preventive war used victimhood as a shield and a sword to justify military intervention in the name of control. This sentiment was best captured in former secretary of state Condoleezza Rice's 2002 quote on CNN that "we don't want the smoking gun to be a mushroom cloud." The discourse of preemptive war fit nicely with the escalation of racist police practices. Led by elites' nationalist sentiments to rally America against a common enemy, a white ethnonationalist sentiment elevated the military and police to heroic and sacred status. From the Tea Party protests against taxes to white mothers tying yellow ribbons around trees in their front yard to the U.S. military sponsoring veteran appreciation moments at sporting events to Blue Lives Matter flags tacked to the bedroom walls and displayed on the front porches of suburban homes to the reemergence of white vigilantism in anti-racist protests, the imprints of white ethnonationalism are all over a new form of white citizenship.

The insurrection at the American Capitol building on January 6, 2021, and the conservative defense of those events illustrate the uneasy but still working alliance between the two forms of white citizenship. The insurrection began at a political rally held by Donald Trump that he titled "Save America." Trump claimed that the Democrats rigged the presidential election and stole it from him, and called on Vice President Mike Pence to nullify the electoral college votes of states that he lost to Joe Biden. Afterward, his supporters marched down the street and stormed the Capitol building. Some broke windows and kicked down doors and scaled walls while others were simply let in the front door. The white rioters had supporters in Congress and on the DC police force. There were other coordinated pro-Trump marches in Los Angeles, Denver, Minneapolis, and even in Salem, Oregon, that same day. The commonality between these events is the centrality of white ethnonational citizenship. We can see this in the dominant white sociological characteristics of white ethnonationalism: the substance of its claims and its style of protest practices. First the claims. White ethnonationalism is about control and understands control as a zero-sum game between whites and racial and ethnic minorities. Much of the conservative rhetoric in politics is wrapped in the aura of elite control, be it state's rights or pro-business labor policy or antiabortion stances. Trump did not create white ethnonational citizenship and it was not Trump's loss per se that triggered this political insurrection. It was the loss of control within the context of anti-racist protests targeting institutions like the police.

The second defining feature of white ethnonationalist citizenship is violence. As Weber noted, politicians are engaged in politics for ideological reasons or to have power for the sake of power, but gaining control of the state gives a political group "the right to use physical force is ascribed to other institutions or to individuals only to the extent to which the state permits it" (Weber 1946, 78). A white ethnonationalist political administration institutionalized and permitted white ethnonationalists to exercise racist violence toward Black citizens. White ethnonationalist violence corresponds to what I have characterized as "figurative violence" elsewhere (Hohle 2013, 2021). Figurative violence refers to how social movements use actual violence and embodied forms of violence to instill fear in their adversaries and inspire their supporters. For one, there is a much longer history of whites using figurative violence in relation to Black America, especially in places where Black people were making economic and political gains. What is unique about twenty-first-century white ethnonationalist citizenship is how white violence, which was originally rooted in nineteenth-century and early twentieth-century civil society, fused into the state, via the police, only to have this fusion undone. This unraveling has, for a lack of a better term, militarized ethnonationalism. White ethnonational violence is more calculated and rational in its deployment. The January 6 insurrectionists used actual violence and physical force to enter the building. The mob killed a police officer. There was white ethnonationalist violence targeting anti-racist protesters, even a situation of a white teenager openly shooting into a crowd and killing an anti-racist protester, during demonstrations against confederate monuments and police brutality. These murders in the name of white ethnonational identification inspire their allies to take whatever means necessary to defend their imaginary white nation. The second feature is the embodiment of the protesters themselves. While much of the media attention was on a white guy dressed up as a wolf, it was a mild distraction from the armed protesters, dressed in military and riot gear, with devices used to take and claim hostages. Combined with the claims of control and use of violence, the embodiments of the white ethnonationalists are cultural signals to their supporters that they are deadly serious in their pursuit to preserve their privileges of American citizenship.

The response from Republicans illustrates how good liberal white citizenship can act as a shield to the white ethnonationalist's sword. In the immediate aftermath of the insurrection, Senate majority leader Mitch McConnell noted that overturning an election would be a "death spiral" for American democracy. He then used his role as Senate minority leader to block the formation of an independent commission, stating that "I do not believe the additional extra venous commission that Democratic leaders want would uncover crucial new facts or promote healing. Frankly, I do not believe it is even designed to do that." One way that good liberal white citizenship acts as a shield is that it does without the theatrics of figurative violence. It favors working within institutions. Good white citizenship has stressed moderation and the politics of respectability since the civil rights era (Kruse 205; Hohle 2012). Although they sought to distance themselves away from bad white citizens and ethnoracial citizens, they inadvertently aligned themselves with white ethnonationalism. Good white citizenship first creates its own symbolic others in the form of bad citizens, and then projects shared racial preferences and bad behaviors onto others that define bad citizenship. Bad citizens are both real and imaginary. The imaginary forms of bad white citizenship have continually been anchored in class and gendered assumptions embodied by the poor uneducated white guy cultural trope. Democrats, liberals, comedians, and many social scientists have fed this assumption. Indeed, all data on the social class of white ethnonationalists point to white professionals and business owners, and include both white men and white women, from the outset. In fact, Trump gained support from white women and lost support from noncollege–educated white men. Whiteness and social class bind these two forms of white citizenship together. Although they sought to distance themselves away from bad white citizens and ethnoracial citizens, they inadvertently aligned themselves with white ethnonationalism. However, as economic inequality between whites continues to expand, white ethnonationalism has emerged as the logical form of white citizenship that will usher in a post-neoliberal political economy.

How does sociospatial practices and housing matter in the relationship between good white citizens and white ethnonationalist citizenship? The emergence of white ethnonationalist citizenship came at a time when residential integration actually declined. A 2021 report by the Othering and Belonging Institute indicated that the residential segregation patterns of segregated places across metropolitan regions continued since the 2010 census. They reported that 81% (169 out of 209) metropolitan regions with at least 200,000 persons were more segregated in 2019 than they were in 1990 (Menendian, Gailes, and Gambhir 2021). More importantly, the report notes that regions with high levels of racially based residential segregation also had high levels of political polarization. Real and virtual communities work with neighborhood-based institutions to shape political preferences. Ethnonationalism found a home in America's suburbs. It was a response to the racial integration of public institutions and public spaces rather than actual neighborhoods or places. Thus, whites' privilege of mobility created the isolated and closed-off segregated white places that sowed subsequent ethnoracial sentiments.

Thus, the remaking and rescaling of urban areas via the neoliberal economy created new concentrations of economic and political power and a site for counter forms of white citizenship to emerge. The white response splintered white-private citizenship into white-private liberal citizenship and white ethnoracial citizenship. Although both forms of white citizenship are a continuation of the neoliberal project, white ethnoracial citizenship stressed a white first political identity. In turn, political alliances were redrawn, as some good white citizens created coalitions with good Black citizens, select aspects of the LGBTQ community, and Asians who reflect the model minority typecast. Ethnoracial white citizens turned inward and rallied around the perceived loss of white control over the political economy. Marginalized Black and Hispanic citizens continued to live on the margins, contrasted to ideals of good citizenship, and outside the domain of whiteness. Many of these struggles for civic inclusion exist at the urban level. These struggles are paradoxical. The struggle for civic inclusion is rooted in the shared experience as urban inhabitants and common demands for collective consumption. However, shared experiences in racially segregated areas, which include all-white areas, produce more social divisions and attempts to capture collective consumption for their groups. The struggle for affordable housing takes place within these larger racial and class systems of citizenship.

The Financialization of Affordable Housing

There are multiple economic factors involved in creating America's housing question. If we had to single out one economic factor responsible for the rise in the cost of housing since the 2000s, it would be the financialization of housing. Financialization refers to the movement of banking and finance into areas of collective consumption for the purposes of pursuing a profit. Financialization occurred in many aspects of collective consumption, including higher education (Cottom 2017), water (Bayliss 2014), electricity (Knuth 2018), and of course, housing (Fields 2015, 2016; Aalbers 2016). Madden and Marcuse explained how the financialization of housing occurred via the mortgage market, first as national and then global banks replaced local lending thrifts, and then through the entry of private equity into the real estate sector after the 2008 Recession (2016, 11–34). Rather than view housing through a social lens of collective consumption, meaning, housing as a home and something to build communities around, the financialization of housing reduced housing to a commodity. In part, housing always had an element of an investment for individuals and families, as well as developers and local governments. The difference is that financialization of housing made housing a commodity for investment banks and private equity groups. Housing markets went from being local and regional in scope to global because capital and its investors are globally based. Their investments are not tied to individuals or families or the well-being of the local community.

The financialization of housing, and really all forms of collective consumption, was made possible because the racial language white-private/black-public created the social conditions for the neoliberal turn. Elite whites and policy makers used the language of white-private to redefine the state's role in creating markets to support white-private businesses, white-private consumers, and the economy as a whole. As I discussed in the previous chapter, the implications for neoliberalism on the fields of social welfare and public housing included austerity, the creation of housing vouchers to create a floor in the private housing market, and decontrolling rent-regulated apartments. The federal government also deregulated the financial field. There was a series of banking deregulations that started in the 1980s and lasted throughout the 1990s that freed investors to enter real estate at levels previously unseen. They included technical changes in lending practices, including the elimination of usury caps in 1980 and the creation of adjustable rate mortgages in 1982 (see Hohle 2018, 92–105). The banking deregulations included removing race as one of the criteria for Small Business Administration support. This transformed Black-owned banks, a small part of the overall financial market that had an outsized impact on providing home mortgages to Black families in local Black neighborhoods, into subprime lending institutions. The result of the banking deregulations in the 1980s culminated in the Savings and Loan Crisis. One part of the story of the Savings and Loan Crisis was the corruption of developers taking out risky loans on the basis that the Federal Savings and Loan Insurance Corporation insurance would cover the losses. In turn, a lot of housing was built in America's sunbelt, especially in Arizona and Texas. The other part of the story is how thrifts, or savings and loans, were transformed into large lending institutions. There were about 4,000 thrifts with about $480 of their $600 billion in total assets tied to mortgages (FDIC 1997). Between regulatory changes that allowed thrifts to introduce adjustable rate mortgages and the corruption of local bankers and developers, the value of assets held by thrifts grew 56% from 1983 to 1985 compared to 24% increase in the value of assets held by banks. The crisis ended with over 1000 thrifts closing due to insolvency and the federal government bailing out the rest in 1989. Rather than change the regulatory field to ensure more stability and weed out corruption, the response to the savings and loan crisis was to open up the real estate market to global competition.

The savings and loan scandal occurred at a time when America and other nations part of the developed world were going through a period of economic transition. America had been undergoing deindustrialization since the 1970s.

American Rust Belt cities, like Pittsburgh, Pennsylvania, began their economic restructuring to a service sector or postindustrial economy prior to the 1980s (Neuman 2016). It didn't matter. The combination of a new economy and cheap housing pulled populations to the sunbelt. However, the transition from an industrial to an information economy created transnational connections between the centers of finance and eventually technology. Recall that one of the basic assumptions of political economy is that the economy creates urban spaces most conducive to the economy. Sassen (1988, 1991) mapped how the neoliberal economy created new global cities. The new global urban networks, characterized as transnational networks because they are centered on the political and economic relationships between cities rather than nation-states, centered the global economy on global finance. It is important to note that the transnational networks did not create centers of global finance, rather, they built on the already existing centers of finance. The transnational networks changed the scale of cities by amplifying the size and scope of urban areas. It is helpful to understand economic globalization through Sassen's transnational lens because she explains how urban areas were remade around high-income sectors, particularly finance, and low-income and low-skilled service workers disproportionately hailing from transnational migrants. This impacts housing in two ways. For one, it creates the conditions for displacement via the restructuring of cities around high-income workers. Second, it creates the conditions for an affordable housing crisis and because the profit-seeking motives of real estate actors are now synced up with global markets. However, if we only focus on these global-level processes and ignore the role of the state and its institutions, we cannot understand how global finance entered local real estate markets and drove up the cost of market rate housing.

A combination of state financial deregulations and institutional changes within the financial sector connected global finance to real estate markets. The diffusion of the neoliberal project in the 1980s led multiple nation-states to change the regulations governing foreign direct investment (Gotham 2006). On a structural level, this made multinational and transnational investments into local housing possible. The flow of global capital into U.S. markets was made easier by a series of U.S. banking deregulations in the 1990s and early 2000s, notably the 1999 Financial Modernization Act that removed legal barriers between commercial and investment banking, and the 2000 Futures Modernization Act that excluded derivatives from being regulated by the Commodities Exchange. On the institutional level the most notable change for housing was the creation of mortgage-backed securities and collateralized debt obligations (Gotham 2006; Fligstein and Habinek 2014). Making a security involves creating a commodity that is standardized but still governed by a set of regulations and shared understandings. For Gotham

(2006), the creation of mortgage-backed securities exemplifies how the state creates liquidity for the real estate market. We can see the need for liquidity for housing investments both on the heels of the savings and loan crisis and the demand for housing as global cities restructured. However, the creation of mortgage-backed securities solved a paradox between the global scope of finance and the local nature of housing markets. Creating a security based on mortgage debt meant that global investment now understood and had a mechanism to invest in any local housing market on the planet. The global scale of the U.S. housing market explains why the financial crisis had such a negative global impact, as so many global financial firms bought and invested in the mortgage-backed securities (Fligstein and Habinek 2014).

The neoliberal state not only created the conditions for speculative investment in the real estate sector, but also actively encouraged it. In their book on the history of financial bubbles, Quinn and Turner focused on the "symbiotic relationship between property developers, banks and politicians" (2020, 189) as the reason for the systemic financial crash of 2008. The American economy looked good on paper during the mid- to late 1990s as speculative investment flowed into technology stocks and private equity into tech start-ups. This created a tech bubble in the stock market that burst in 2000, erasing $1.75 trillion in the market value of technology stocks. This triggered another recession. The state's response to the 2001 Recession was a combination of tax cuts for the wealthy and the federal reserve lowering interest rates. The goal was to stimulate the economy by increasing demand in the housing and real estate sector. Consolidation in the banking and home builder sectors was already underway in the 1990s. This left fewer and fewer local builders and local banks who had local knowledge of local housing markets. Financial institutions reacted to these state and industry changes by creating new forms of consumer mortgages. The new forms of consumer lending were exotic mortgages, such as no money down, or interest-only payments for the first 10 years, or introductory or teaser rates that increased after a 5- or 7-year period. The practice of actually finding and lending money to would-be homebuyers and existing homeowners looking to refinance to a lower interest involved predatory lending in the subprime market. Financial firms then packaged subprime loans and sold them as mortgage-backed securities, which, up until the late 1990s, were an otherwise conservative investment. The reason why they were a conservative investment was that the overwhelming majority of mortgages packaged into a security were prime rate mortgages amortized over a 30-year period. The risk of default was low. Furthermore, harking back to one of reasons why the savings and loan crisis was systemic, the subprime mortgages were insured by companies like AIG and the Mortgage Guaranty Insurance Corporation. The sheer number of mortgage defaults was too much for the insurance companies to handle.

America's response to the 2008 Recession inadvertently expanded the affordable housing crisis to all urban areas. There were two state responses of note that were particularly troublesome. The first response was that the state bailed out the banks. Why did the state bail out the banks but not the homeowners? I am not suggesting that the state should have not bailed out the banks. I am suggesting that the state should have bailed out homeowners by mandating banks refinance subprime mortgages so that homeowners could have remained in their home. The answer to the question is found in the racial composition of the subprime market and the institutional practice of predatory lending. Just as the already existing financial centers make transnational networks and global cities possible, the already existing fact of residential segregation made the institutionalization of predatory lending and subprime lending possible. Because of residential segregation, Rugh and Massey (2010) noted that financial firms treated Black clients differently, evidenced by the number of subprime mortgages issued to Black borrowers, and that foreclosures were higher in predominantly Black neighborhoods than white neighborhoods. Subprime lending accounted for a 43% increase in Black homeownership in the 1990s. By 1998, 51% of the total dollar amount of subprime loans was issued in Black neighborhoods, and 58% of subprime refinanced loans were made in predominantly Black neighborhoods. In comparison, 10% of subprime refinanced loans were made in predominantly white neighborhoods (Hohle 2018, 99). Subprime lending represented a new application of racism through housing. Whereas Black families used to be denied mortgages, banks now granted Black family's mortgages on the basis of exploitation through higher interest rates.

The second response was how the banks sold off the foreclosed homes. Not only were 8.7 million jobs lost because of the recession, more than 8-million homes were foreclosed on, and another 95 million homes lost equity. This created a problem of volume for banks. Banks had to unload a lot of homes in a very short period of time. There was also the problem of zombie homes, homes that were foreclosed on and vacated by the homeownership, but no one could or would acknowledge legal ownership of the house. Zombie homes are a detriment to communities because no one does the upkeep on the home and no one is paying property taxes. The solution to this problem was to pool foreclosed homes together into a single auction rather than sell each house individually. Calhoun (2018) noted that this was the point that brought in hedge funds and private equity into the private housing market. They were the only two actors with enough liquid capital to purchase pools of homes that numbered in the 100s. While this was a more efficient way to get the housing supply back on the market, it changed the character of the rental market and the local neighborhood. We can also think of the auctioning of pools of foreclosed homes as starting a second wave of financialization of housing.

Whereas the first wave of financialization was the entry of finance into the housing market via securities, the second wave was the direct entry into the housing market via the ownership of housing units. Private equity firms became landlords. Private equity firms like Blackstone created a subsidiary, Invitation Homes, that manages about 80,000 housing units (Mari 2020). In 2021, they bought 66 multifamily buildings that provided 5,800 affordable housing units in San Diego for $1 billion. By 2019, private equity owned about 250,000 single-family homes and about 1 million apartment units, valued between $40 and $60 billion (Americans for Financial Reform 2020).

At no point in this never-ending cycle of crisis and response caused by the financialization of housing has the state acted in a way that understood housing as something other than a commodity or an investment or as a means to drive economic growth. So long as the problem of affordable housing was a problem associated with Black and other racial and ethnic minorities, it was not a matter of public and national concern. As the affordable housing problem diffused to the white middle classes and threatened to undermine macroeconomic growth, the only solution offered by elite politicians and developers and government officials was to find a way to build more market rate housing. Although the racial language of white-private does not appear at every point in the twenty-first-century American housing question, it created the foundational policy framework for the financialization of housing to operate off of and continues to create a cultural framework that limits the solution to the housing problem.

What Can We Learn from the Case Study of the Financialization of Housing and the State's Response to the 2008 Housing Crisis?

There are two important inferences to make regarding the financialization of housing. The first is that financialization of housing created two housing bubbles. If we glance at table 5.1, the period of the savings and loan scandal that technically spanned from 1980 to 1995, but especially at the peak years between 1982 and 1989, increased the number of completed new housing units. A similar uptick is apparent from 2001 to 2006, before the number of new completed housing declined sharply into the start of the Great Recession. This points to the economic paradox at the heart of the affordable housing problem: you cannot separate speculation and profit-seeking motives from increasing the supply of housing in the private housing market. History indicates that increases in the supply of market rate housing accompany an increase in the actors looking to profit from housing. This involved the entry of private equity firms directly into the real estate market as landlords rather than as holders of mortgage-backed securities. It involved exploitative lending practices to sell homes to Black individuals and families. The current

Black homeownership rate of 41.6% has reverted back to levels not seen since the 1960s. In comparison, the white homeownership rate was still a healthy 72.9% (Calhoun 2018). This was not a racially neutral housing market or recovery. Any attempt to increase the supply of market rate housing via a supply side stimulus will inevitably create a housing bubble—unless there is an increase in the supply of housing in the public housing market and unless steps are taken to eliminate speculative investing from the private housing field (figure 5.1).

The second inference we can make is how the combination of race, financialization, and globalization created distant proximate fields between global and local housing private housing markets, but parallel fields between private and public housing markets. The banking deregulations that led to the financialization of housing tied the primary and secondary circuits of capital together. Although larger urban regions and systems have formed around the centers of finance and technology, the type of housing that gets built is still predominantly large single-family housing. Developers are building new homes in the outer suburbs or luxury apartments in the city centers because they are the most profitable types of new housing. The type of housing needed to supply affordable housing in large metropolitan areas, whether or not they are characterized as being dense or sprawled, are not being constructed. Both types of housing overwhelmingly end up going to high-income white individuals or families. There are urban inhabitants who have high incomes who endure affordable housing. They are considered cost burdened. There are also urban inhabitants who endure the low-skilled and low-wage labor market. They are severely cost burdened. The only similarity they share is the cost of housing exceeds 30% a month of their income.

There is no public housing field to act as a proximate field to the private housing field. Nor is there a meaningful supply of rent-regulated apartments in America's largest urban regions of New York and Los Angeles. As noted in the last chapter, the era of America's public housing experiment basically ended with the 1999 Fairclough Amendment that capped the maximum number of fixed public housing units that local governments could build. The state's response to the postrecession affordable housing problem was to double down on privatization of public housing. In 2012, Housing and Urban Development (HUD) created the Rental Assistance Demonstration (RAD) that permitted public housing agencies to convert dilapidated public housing into long-term project-based privately owned housing. It also provided funding to private housing that are in need of maintenance and participates in the Section 8 program. RAD capped the number of public housing units that could be converted into private affordable housing at 400,000. The conversion of public to Section 8 housing does increase the number of housing units in the field of public housing, but it does create more rental units for landlords to profit off of.

New Privately Owned Housing Units, Completed, United States, 1980-2020
(Housing Units in Thousands)

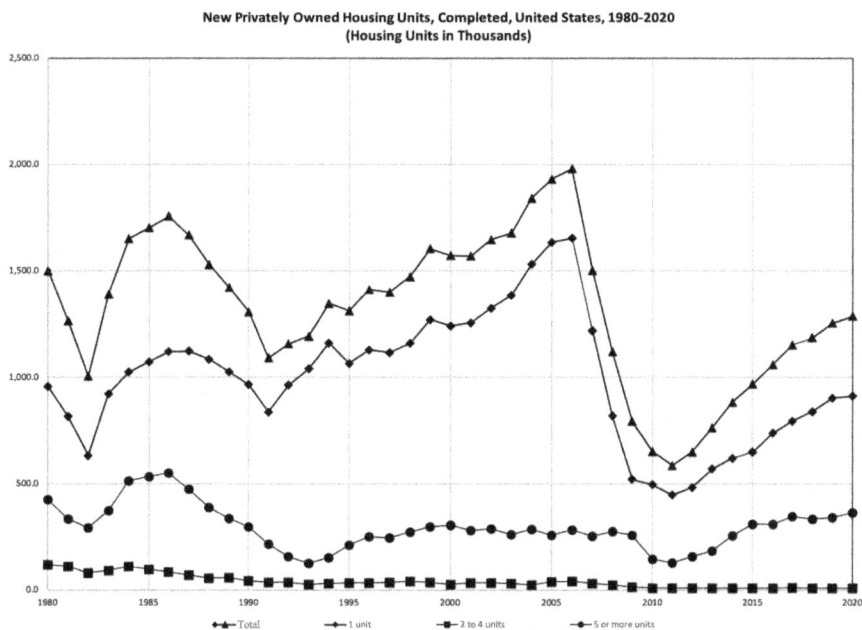

Figure 5.1 New Privately Owned Housing Units, Completed, United States, 1980–2020.
Source: US Census, New Residential Construction https://www.census.gov/construction/nrc/index.html

Furthermore, given the limited amount of supply of Section 8 vouchers relative to the demand, especially in expensive urban areas, converting public housing to private Section 8 accepting housing is not the answer. It is an extension of longer-term mistakes of following austerity with privatization.

The implication of the financialization of housing and the creation of distinct housing fields is that it represents a shift in the privilege of mobility. Similar to the turn of the twentieth century, the private housing market is basically the luxury housing market. Today's wealthy whites have exercised a historic form of white privilege to create racially and class homogenous communities. This is the housing market financed by global capital and elite developers. The limited supply of affordable housing for the white middle classes has relegated them to a form of mobility that sits somewhere between elite whites and Black citizens. The white middle classes are mobile and not contained in racially segregated housing markets and neighborhoods like Black citizens are. But the state no longer supplies the conditions for all-whites to avoid the problem of affordable housing, including displacement. Are America's urban social movements up to the task of securing affordable housing for everyone, or will it succumb to the logic of preserving the privilege of elite white mobility at the expense of other racial and ethnic minorities? That is the question we'll explore now.

URBAN SOCIAL MOVEMENTS AND THE AFFORDABLE HOUSING SOLUTIONS

Political elites and the real estate sector are not going to provide affordable housing because of an op-ed article in a national newspaper or a social media post or a book or a study by a think tank laying out the society-wide benefits of affordable housing. If America is going to implement real affordable housing initiatives, it will be because today's urban social movements create the political conditions to do so. Only actors working within the affordable housing field can change the logic and decisions over affordable housing policy to reflect the needs of ordinary citizens rather than capital. This means changing how we use land, changing who housing is built for, and thinking about housing as a social good rather than as a commodity. And it is not just in policy itself. Mobilizing across spaces at the urban level allows for urban social movements to define a form of urban citizenship around inhabitants regardless of their legal status or racial makeup. It could potentially have national ramifications that lead to America embracing the public and redefining national citizenship around a real egalitarian framework. However, as I have argued in this book, the only way to find a solution is to be mindful that affordable housing policy has privileged white mobility over providing actual affordable housing units. The problems of racism and mobility remain even in liberal and well-meaning struggles for affordable housing in the early twenty-first century.

Contemporary housing movements emphasize balancing affordability with increasing the housing supply. Phillips (2020) synthesized the broad goals of affordable housing activists into three dimensions: supply, stability, and subsidy. Supply is building enough housing units for everyone. Stability is understanding that housing also means that residents have access to other forms of collective consumption, such as clean and safe neighborhoods and decent schools, and that housing is more than just an economic investment. Subsidy is about providing subsidized housing, through rental assistance or some form of subsidized housing. This synthesis is important because it begins to overcome the tensions that exist between tenant protections and public rental subsidies and the supply of market rate housing found in the affordable housing debates (see chapter 2). For example, Phillips shows us that San Francisco's affordable housing problems are mired in a pro-tenant but anti-housing approach. While the city offers strong protections for existing renters, there is powerful and widespread opposition from Not In My

BackYard (NIMBY) groups over constructing new housing. This created a housing shortage. On the other hand, places like Austin, Texas, are pro-housing but anti-tenant. Unlike California, Texas has an ample supply of cheap land and no rent regulations. This means that homeownership is a real possibility for middle-income Texans, but low-income Texans still endure high rents and higher-than-average eviction rates, and that homeownership has come at the expense of environmental degradation due to urban sprawl. Embracing a pro-tenant and pro-housing approach is a way out of this afford-able housing problem.

Even though I like Phillips's approach to synthesizing the various threads of housing movements, there are real limits to the solutions in the current affordable housing synthesis. First, it assumes that high real estate prices and rents are due to scarcity rather than the logic of the second circuit of capital-ism (Phillips 2020, 19). Second, the increase in housing supply, even when the supply is ample like in Texas, is limited to upper-income and middle-income whites. In Texas, like other sunbelt states, white mobility through twenty-first-century sprawling suburban homeownership looks an awful lot like mid-twentieth-century sprawling suburban homeownership in New Jersey. Therefore, I want to look at two movements that address affordable housing. The first are the YIMBY movements focused on increasing the sup-ply of housing units. The second are the local housing movements that mobi-lize through Community Land Trusts (CLTs). As I will show, despite their promises, both fall in the trap to using affordable housing to maintain racial segregation, one by championing white mobility through the market and the other by using land trusts to preserve racial segregation paradoxically in the guise of protecting residential displacement.

Urban Citizenship and Varieties of YIMBYism

The urban social movement that has received the most public and scholarly attention since the end of the 2008 Recession is the YIMBY movement. One question is whether or not this is an actual urban social movement, a serious social movement, or just a case of real estate elites forming alliances with upper-middle-class whites. I find it useful to think of YIMBYism as a hous-ing movement in a broader pro-development field. Strategic action fields are the arenas of modern political and economic life defined by mesoac-tions, like sociospatial practices, which are embedded in broader urban and economic systems. A YIMBY movement is part of a strategic action field that is either competing with or working with other political and economic actors over the use and meaning of urban space. YIMBY movements are a type of urban social movement that appeals to market forces to solve urban problems. A YIMBY movement's solution to the affordable housing solution is straightforward: if we increase the supply of housing units then the price of housing will go down. Their proposed solution is found in deregulating zoning laws to permit the construction of new private market homes. What is not exactly straightforward is how the supply of new housing units will reach those at the lower-income end of the affordability spectrum. Old housing units are not filtering down and the recent decades of wage stagnation suggest that urban inhabitants are not practicing up-renting like economists predict (Masts 2019). Nor is it entirely clear how the real estate sector is supposed to increase the supply of housing units independently of its profit and rent-seeking investors.

The origins of YIMBY movements date back to the 1980s. It was a catch-all phrase used by urbanists to capture how local residents mobilized against NIMBY opposition to new projects, like drug treatment facilities, detention centers, homeless shelters, and affordable housing (Brown and Glanz 2018). The acronym entered the public lexicon after housing justice activists in California's Bay Area began using the phrase in response to the region's affordable housing problem around 2014 (Brown and Glanz 2018; Shaw 2018; Gates 2020; Dougherty 2020). The global technology sector is concentrated in the Bay Area. This includes some of the world's largest tech companies, like Google, Apple, and Facebook. The technology sector attracts high-skilled workers and high-paying jobs to the area. Venture capitalists followed the networks from Stanford University to Silicon Valley in hopes of profiting from the next disruptive technology. Not many places have or have had the problem of too many good paying jobs and lots of outside investment capital. Other urban regions that were also the winners in the neoliberal economy dominated by finance and technology experienced similar problems. But this becomes a problem when the economic growth of an urban region is captured by elites, and housing is either no longer built for ordinary middle class and poor inhabitants, or built at all.

YIMBY solutions to the affordable housing problem are to deregulate existing zoning laws that prevent the construction of new market rate housing. It is the emphasis on deregulating the market that gives YIMBYs its neoliberal designation. Given that geographical and economic and sociological differences exist between urban regions, it is sometimes more helpful to think of the varieties of YIMBYism rather than view the movement as just focusing on market rate housing. By varieties of YIMBYism, I mean conceptualizing YIMBY movements more broadly, as pro-development movements, where the meaning of development is determined by its spatial context and its sociospatial practices. YIMBY movements differ by their spatial context because each urban region presents its own unique barrier to housing and development. For example, California has a lot of land to build housing, but that land is zoned for single-family housing. Seattle, Washington, has the same restrictive zoning ordinance, as well as restrictions on building heights. New York City has built new housing, but it has been mostly luxury housing for the wealthy global elite. In America's Rust Belt, the affordable housing problems are tied to constructing the type of housing that planners and government officials think will attract outside capital investment and to rebuild their city centers. The Sunbelt, in contrast, has ample space to build housing and an appetite to build. However, they generally have no tenant protections and new housing has meant sprawl. One problem of taking a narrow slice of California's Bay Area's housing problem and generalizing that single condition as the reason why housing is not affordable everywhere is that the price of housing has increased whether local areas are building housing or not. In other words, depending on where the YIMBY movement is located, their one-size-fits-all slogan of "build baby build" is neither a full nor a partial solution to America's housing question.

In addition to looking at the varieties of YIMBYism, we can generally divide YIMBY movements into two ideal types. Each ideal type is defined in relation to a core feature of urban citizenship: inclusion and exclusion. The first ideal type is exclusionary YIMBYism. Exclusionary YIMBYism draws from a normative ideal of good white citizenship. It is housing for high-income whites who feel as if they are being cheated out of a home despite their history of controlling the things that they can control, such as increasing their educational attainment to leverage high-paying jobs. In turn, the sociospatial practices of exclusionary YIMBYism focus on the general issue of affordability that impacts high-income workers. This sentiment is best captured in supporters, such as Conor Dougherty (2020), who take their intellectual cue from Edward Glaeser's critique of zoning laws. Dougherty's approach to affordable housing policy is rooted in ensuring white mobility is possible to "high-mobility places":

> The ability to move to a high-opportunity city is a huge and vastly underrated piece of how societies get richer. Growing cities tend to have the highest economic mobility, and there's plenty of data and common sense to support the idea that people's lives can be vastly improved by going from a place that doesn't have much work to a place that has a lot of it. (Dougherty 2020, xv)

From this perspective, the best way to accomplish this is to increase the supply of market rate housing so that high-income individuals and families can afford to purchase a home.

On the other end of the YIMBY political continuum are the inclusionary YIMBY movements. Inclusionary YIMBY movements argue that urban areas need to pair efforts to increase the supply of new housing with tenant protections. Inclusionary YIMBYism is a marginalized aspect of the YIMBY movement. Its origins are found in housing activists working on the front lines attempting to bridge the need for inclusionary tenant protections with the dominant pro-market fundamentalist YIMBY faction. The inclusionary YIMBY sentiment, captured by Randy Shaw (2018), rejects the binary between increasing new market housing and offering tenant protections in the form of rent control, anti-rent gouging, and just cause evictions laws. Shaw argued that when this false antimony between market housing and tenant protections is in place, it creates the political conditions for left-wing groups to reject YIMBY movements on the ground that they are "developer shills" (2018, xx) on the basis that new market housing creates displacement. Unlike the exclusionary versions of YIMBYism, Shaw acknowledges the negative role new HUD has had on the local Black population in Oakland and Latino population in Texas. However, Shaw is pretty silent on the how and why the exclusionary YIMBY movement can adopt tenant protections into their assumptions. It is one of the problems of the inequality of ideas within a field: the groups in subordinate positions within the field appeal to the group in the dominant position, but in the process, reorganize their position and practice to reflect the dominant group's standpoint. His rendition of inclusionary YIMBYism is left demanding flexibility from both so-called liberal and other left-wing housing groups that reject new market rate housing and from neoliberal housing groups that reject subsidized low-income housing and other tenant protections. What is kept in place is the core belief that the market is capable of supplying housing, as long as we build enough of it.

The limit of YIMBY movements is that they inadvertently build from existing sociospatial inequalities rather than outright replacing them. As I stated earlier in the book, it is demanding a right to the housing market rather than a right to housing. Building a housing movement on the foundation of good white citizenship means organizing a housing movement around the trust and reliance on the market to solve housing problems. The assumption is that all class and racial groups have the same access to the housing market as upper-middle-class whites. This assumption would make sense if it were not for pesky reality of residential segregation and an unequal labor market characterized by racial discrimination, gender discrimination, and historical wage stagnation. The assumptions that zoning deregulations can fix the problems of racial segregation or displacement reduce racism to a technical problem and as an outcome of policy. What have zoning deregulations done? Zoning deregulations have led to more housing, just not housing for the middle classes and the poor. It has served as a means for global elites and the wealthy to capture a monopoly over rental and housing prices because they have the excess capital to sit on housing. They can set the price of housing and rents and wait until that price is met—even if it means sitting on empty units. The entire YIMBY model relies on the assumption of filter down housing, which in practice, does not occur, at least it does not occur outside of homes for the wealthy filtering down to homes for the rich.

As I have argued in this book, housing and the epistemic privilege of housing policy is the outcome of the political struggle between racial and class groups. The market follows this lead. Inclusionary YIMBY movements have good intentions, but their focus on stopping displacement comes at the expense of the continued marginalization of those in need of housing. The inclusive YIMBY solution builds on existing racial and sociospatial inequalities rather than in spite of them. The reason why is that racism creates a paradox at the heart of affordable housing and both ideal type YIMBY movements. Tenant protections create the conditions for poor Black and other racial and ethnic minorities to remain in larger metropolitan regions, but it does so at the cost of maintaining racial segregation. Rather than creating the conditions for marginalized urban inhabitants to exercise a right to mobility, they are contained in sections of urban regions that elites allow them to inhabit. A city or urban region cannot be inclusive if it remains fundamentally segregated by race. In the end, YIMBYs state the obvious, that we need more housing, but other than that, they are short on ideas and evidence that just increasing the supply of market rate housing will change much of anything.

Community Land Trusts

One of the main problems of affordable housing is that the value of real estate increases at a much faster pace than wages. The reason why is that the economic value of real estate comes from speculation and profit-seeking actors who are looking to make money by capturing rents. Urban social movements have mobilized through CLTs as a way to tame the second circuit of capital and establish permanent places for affordable housing. The use of CLTs is not a common strategy to provide affordable housing. There were a little more than 225 CLTs in the United States in 2018 (HUD 2019). It is an uncommon strategy because it requires local governments working with community groups instead of with real estate developers. However, CLTs provide a way out of the trap of the second circuit of capital: increasing the supply of housing increases the cost of land which increases the cost of housing.

CLTs are a system of tenure where the ownership of land is separate from the ownership of the buildings or housing structures. There are two main actors involved in the CLT: the nonprofit or CBO and the residents. The land is owned by a nonprofit and an individual or family owns the housing structures. The CBO typically purchases the land, although there are examples of a city using eminent domain to acquire land for the CLT (Meehan 2014). Members of the community and government officials jointly manage the CBO overseeing the CLT. CLTs cause no additional financial burden to cities. All parties involved continue to pay property and real estate taxes. Homeowners also pay small membership fees to the CLT. This is not the same system that fleeces local communities out of tax revenue, like organized religion and churches and some not-for-profit organizations do. The real value of CLTs is that they are set up to prevent real estate from being used as a means of profit and rent seeking. Since the CLT owns the land and essentially removes it from the private market, it prevents land speculation. It does so by building strict regulations into the land lease and homeowner agreements. These regulations cap how much a homeowner can sell their housing unit. The CLT typically has the right to repurchase the home and resell it to another family in need of housing. In some cities, there are also strict income requirements that limit who can purchase the homes to those making less than the area's median incomes. Combined, capital cannot invest in land or the structures. Since the values of homes are not just tied to labor and materials, there is no way for housing costs to rise suddenly or to exceed the rise of income over time.

The history of social movements using CLTs to provide housing originated in the civil rights movement and in rural areas. CLTs drew from a long-standing idea found in enlightenment thinkers like John Stuart Mill and the American political economist Henry George that land should be used for the common good (Davis 2014). The modern use of a CLT dates to 1969, after a group of activists that belonged to the Black civil rights movement in Albany, Georgia. The origins of the Albany Movement date back to 1961. Members of SNCC worked with Albany's local Black elites to desegregate the entire city rather than select public institutions, as was the case in Montgomery. Martin Luther King Jr. arrived at Albany in hopes of bringing national media attention to the small Georgia city. Local Sheriff Laurie Pritchett had other ideas. Pritchett countered King's good black citizenship with good white policing, pitting his racially nonthreatening police who were instructed to refrain from violence against the racially nonthreatening demonstrators. The national media showered Pritchett with praise. King left, but the movement did not end. Local SNCC activists continued their struggle for equality (see Hohle 2013, 69–73). One result was the movement created a CLT to house and protect the property rights of Black farmers. CLTs did not find a home in urban areas until the 1970s and 1980s, as newly elected Socialist mayors in Santa Monica, Santa Cruz, and Berkeley, California, as well as Burlington, Vermont, worked with community groups to acquire land for the purposes of creating affordable housing (Soifer 1990). Organizers formed CLTs in large urban areas and midsized cities throughout the 1990s and into the 2000s in response to the need for affordable housing.

CLTs are a modern-day alternative to public housing and rent regulations. For one, they are able to replicate the organizational form and vision of public housing. Recall from chapter 3 that public housing was originally set up to provide decent and safe and sanitary housing for the working poor and working class as an alternative to the slums. Public housing tenants paid fees or rent to offset the cost of maintenance. In addition to serving on the CLT governing board and attending community meetings, the presence of a financial incentive or fee creates a personal stake in the CLT that is not found in renting. Theoretically, a CLT does not place any restrictions on mobility. A homeowner or family that resides in a CLT is free to sell their structure and relocate if their financial or family situation changes, or really, for whatever reason they want. Similar to rent regulations, the objective of CLTs is to place a soft price cap on the resale value of the land. In California, CLTs were used with other tenant protections, notably rent control, in a comprehensive approach to place some sort of price caps to counter the increased cost of housing. Similar to rent control, CLTs install a price cap on how much the price of housing can increase in a given year or time period. This keeps the cost of housing in line with household income. What makes the CLT different is that it emphasizes homeownership and is not a program that only benefits whites. Homeownership involves the social aspects of housing that ties an individual and family to a community. It provides stability and sustainability. It provides some means to create wealth for working people of color rather than generate income for a landlord. Although CLTs will not eliminate the racial wealth gap on its own, it can be part of the solution.

TOWARD A SOLUTION TO THE AMERICAN HOUSING QUESTION

CLTs offer a lot of potential to solve the American housing question. The biggest advantage of CLTs is that they can create a proximate field of affordable housing that can work with the private housing market. In order to do this, community groups and local municipalities have to learn from the limitations of YIMBY movements and recognize that CLTs cannot be a continuation of affordable housing policy that prioritizes the white privilege of mobility. While CLTs have focused on removing the speculative investment in the housing market, they have not maximized the quantity of housing on the land trusts. One reason why is that some CLTs view homeownership through the lens of a single-family home. However, a more significant issue that CLTs face is that CBOs do not have the capacity to raise the necessary amount of private capital to undertake a large endeavor like developing multiunit housing complexes. But the state does have the capacity to invest public capital into large-scale CLT developments. To the critic, the idea of the state constructing large-scale housing units is nothing more than a return to fixed public housing. My guess is that the image in the critic's mind is Pruitt-Igoe.

That's an image wrapped in a language of Black-public. The critics should be thinking about modern-day condominiums.

If CLTs and YIMBY movements do not address the issue of racism, both will succumb to the trap of the affordable housing policy. The trap is that affordable housing policy has historically emphasized white mobility rather than actually providing affordable housing units. White mobility is relational to Black immobility. Dealing with the role of land and real estate speculation is important but it does not address the problem of racial segregation. Racial segregation works differently through CLTs and YIMBY movements. As noted earlier, YIMBY movements' reliance on the market excludes Black and other racial and ethnic minorities who face racial discrimination in the private housing field. The paradox found in real and existing CLTs is that it preserves racial segregation as means of fighting displacement. In part this is because CLTs are no longer connected with its historical Socialist framework that views property and land-based relationships or land redistribution as fundamental to creating a class structure. But mostly it is because CLTs also fall victim to the white mobility/Black immobility binary. The contemporary CLT works through the language of white-private. Like other forms of neo-liberal social welfare, CLTs are privatized through the nonprofit sector and work through the structure of a public-private partnership whose objective is urban revitalization or what Davis (1984) referred to as equity reallocation. CLTs are overwhelmingly formed in Black neighborhoods that are not attractive to private capital. The CLT provides the option for Black and other racial and ethnic minorities to secure affordable housing on the condition that the neighborhood remains segregated from the surrounding gentrified or developing areas. They conflate preventing displacement with meaningful forms of civic inclusion.

Racism remains the biggest obstacle to solving America's housing question. One way to address this is to take the model of a CLT and geographically scale it across the metropolitan region. Although the central city holds a lot of symbolic value, we cannot equate the city with the urban. The state can use public capital to construct the housing units and sell them to residents who make less than a given income based on the threshold of the metropolitan region. Existing CLTs have used the threshold of 80% of the area's median income. The cost of housing can be capped at 150% of a specified area's median income. Rather than worrying about the economic efficiencies of a family bettering their lot in life and choosing to remain in CLT-governed housing units, think of the social benefits of stability and sustainability that accompany mixed-class and mixed-race neighborhoods.

Although racism is the biggest obstacle to solving America's housing question, we cannot overlook the way that racism changed the social meanings and value of public and private, and how this prevents new ways of thinking about affordable housing. It is as if elite and ordinary whites are only capable of envisioning affordable housing solutions through the private market and the private housing vouchers, even though both are subsidized and propped up by public capital. European countries have used the state and public capital to provide for social housing. This has not had a negative impact on homeownership rates, as both France and Germany have homeownership rates north of 50% (Tusell 2017). In fact, the problem of affordable housing in Europe arose with increased immigration to the city centers and the subsequent privatization of some of its social housing stock. Some countries have responded with a CLT model, also called "surface rights," that ensures the land remains public while an individual or family has the right to inhabit the structures. In the end, if America wants to solve its affordable housing problem or move on from the neoliberal project, it must simultaneously deal with America's original problem of racism.

Conclusion

RECLAIMING THE VALUE OF PUBLIC

This book is a critique of democracy more so than a critique of capitalism. When I ask the question of whether or not it is possible to reclaim the value of public in a multiethnic and multiracial society, it is a critique of democratic institutions like civil society and citizenship. In theory, democratic institutions create the conditions for civic inclusion and freedom and equal opportunity. The dark side of democratic institutions is that they exclude others, either by design or because of the assumptions of who and what counts as good citizenship—the basis of civic inclusion—is silenced in the normal workings of democracy. T. H. Marshall's (1964) key insight to twentieth-century citizenship was that it provided a foundation of equality for subsequent forms of inequality to be built upon. Ruth Lister (1997) noted that the able-bodied male not only served as the symbolic assumption behind notions of liberal and republican citizenship, but the very notion of public life was built on the suppression of women and the private sphere of the family. Bell (1980, 1987), Crenshaw (1989), and Delgado and Stefancic (2001) all developed theories of how racism operates through juridical systems based on the shared insight that legal institutions work to preserve the rights and privileges of good whites. In other words, the public was made possible by creating a notion of good citizenship and setting it in relation to either bad or second-tier forms of citizenship.

Good white citizenship was baked into housing policy. Although white and Black citizens fought for the right to housing, New Deal era housing policy ensured that housing went to whites. Not only was public housing racially segregated, the municipal housing agencies also screened applicants and installed behavior codes of conduct to guarantee that they awarded housing to good whites, and to a limited extent, good Black families. However, housing policy also created the conditions for good whites at first, then all-whites, to enjoy the privilege of mobility. The privilege of mobility made good white citizenship work with supply side approaches to subsidize private housing. The democratic institutions created to grant whites the rights and privileges of American citizenship meant denying Black individuals and families the same right to mobility. The civil rights movement was a movement for racial inclusion. This included housing. Elite whites with the growing support of ordinary whites responded to Black civic inclusion by jettisoning their support for the public.

The most troubling paradox about the American welfare state is that it only came into existence when the benefits of citizenship were restricted to whites. That was the age of white-public. It included housing. Since the civil rights era, elite whites have devalued the notion of the public in order to advance the neoliberal project. They found their support in ordinary whites, who worked with and through segregationist groups, and shared elite whites' desire to maintain racial inequality. When whites lost the fight to keep schools and public places racially segregated, they focused on segregating urban regions, and experimented with affordable housing policy to ensure whites maintained their privilege of mobility. Privatization emerged as the key means to achieve this: the private housing voucher let whites move to places beyond their economic means, just as school vouchers allowed white families to send their children to private schools that are beyond their economic means. The privilege of mobility is an escape clause for ordinary whites. For elite whites, privatization as a policy preference meant controlling the distribution of public capital, and ultimately to profit from collective consumption. America's twenty-first-century housing question is one effect of the neoliberal project.

As I noted in the introduction, one of the goals of this book was to reclaim the subjugated value of public. In part, I meant reclaiming the value of the public from its neoliberal deterrents. But I also meant from George himself. Henry George was a racist. In the process of creating a concept of the public to counter the 19th form of privatization, particularly how privately owned land created monopolies over rent was responsible for inequality, George may have been the first to articulate a language of white-public. George wanted publicly controlled land, utilities, transportation, and a universal basic income. He supported women's suffrage. He also believed that the only way to achieve all of this was to restrict the benefits to whites. He targeted Chinese and Black citizens, the latter were still enslaved by elite whites only a few years prior to George becoming a public intellectual.[1] Whereas Engels's housing question could only be solved by workers securing the means of production, George's housing question was partially solved by the Chinese question: removing Chinese citizens and immigrants from American soil. George never directly stated why it was necessary to expel Chinese Americans from the country or why claiming that Black citizens were unlearned and barbarians was a necessary presumption to his theory that became known as Georgism. But he didn't have to. In that era, every social movement was basically all-white—the populists, labor movements, women's suffrage, the progressive movement—and advocating for rights or using public capital for the public good was successful when it was limited to the good of the white-public.

Can color-blind or race-neutral housing policies provide real affordable housing options for twenty-first-century America? The answer to this question rests more on the racial meanings associated with the concept of public than it does just on the racial inequities pertaining to the distribution of resources. Not only do color-blind or race-neutral social and housing policies disproportionately benefit whites, but also the necessary condition to make them a reality is a given degree of white belief in the value of the public. This is not just the case for neoliberal housing policy. It also holds true for leftist and Socialist policy preferences. For example, let us consider how two Socialist-inspired tax policies, one that originates from George himself and a second championed by contemporary economists who specialize in taxation—the Land Value Tax (LVT), a wealth tax, and a progressive income tax—would work when we exclude the race of the actors involved and assume a color-blind meaning of public.

The LVT taxes land but not the structures on the land. In theory, the LVT provides an economic incentive to efficiently use and develop land and prevents economic gains created by labor from being sucked up by the real estate sector. The exact amount of the LVT is based on the gap that exists between the realized and unrealized value of the land. Because an LVT does not tax the structure on the land, the tax is constant whether or not it sits empty, has a single house on it, has a multi-housing unit structure on it, or is developed into commercial real estate. As the value of urban land increases, so does the LVT. That way, public investments are always recouped by the public. The LVT is designed to force landowners and developers to develop vacant or unused land rather than sit on it for tax purposes or because wealthy landowners have enough capital on hand to buy and hold land—two practices that are the basis for real estate speculation and the second circuit of capital. What type of land is subject to a land tax? Historically, empty urban lots were the target of this tax. You could add surface parking lots, a waste of land in city centers and suburban business and retail districts, to the list. However, a twenty-first-century land tax would target housing that is used as investment, including housing units placed in the house sharing market, that is, Airbnb, or sits empty as investors wait for the price to increase, rather than housing that is used as a home. The public capital generated from the land wealth tax is either redistributed back to the community in the form of a universal basic income, or used to build and maintain public infrastructure, such as transportation, greed spaces, and telecommunications.

A second way to make housing more affordable is to increase income so the monthly rent to income ratio decreases. This means increasing the share of income that goes to workers by reinstituting a progressive tax and tax on capital. This way of thinking about the housing question is rooted in Engels's thought process about the redistribution of economic gains to all workers. The most direct way to address economic inequality and income distribution is through taxation. As Saez and Zucman (2019) point out, a global tax avoidance industry helped transform America's progressive tax into a giant flat tax. The ultra-wealthy pays about 20% of its income into taxes, compared with the rest of America that pays between 25% and 30% of its income in taxes. Low taxes are the result of economic inequality because the wealthy use their political power to decide what to tax, how to tax it, and the levels of taxation on high earners. Unsurprisingly, this led to a system of tax evasion and avoidance, where the wealthy avoid income taxes and lower taxes on capital, for example, corporate income and property taxes. The combination of low taxes on capital and the system of tax evasion surrounding real estate creates the conditions for speculative capital investments into the private housing field, while also decreasing the amount of public investments necessary for a robust public housing field. The LVT addresses the tax avoidance on capital taxation. Economists specializing in economic inequality and taxation have proposed two solutions to address economic inequality—both would have a positive indirect effect on housing. The first is installing the optimal tax rate of 83% on high earners (Piketty, Saez, and Stantcheva 2014). Piketty, Saez, and Stantcheva arrived at an optimal tax rate of 83% on high earners by taking into account how levels of taxation affect the supply of high earner's labor, tax avoidance, and their use of different forms of compensation in place of income. Lower capital taxes create the situation for CEOs to monopolize profits and avoid taxes. An optimal tax rate of 83% on higher earners means that even if profits from firms are funneled to the rich, it is taxed away and becomes public capital that can be reinvested into UBI programs or used in place of regressive taxes, like the sales tax or a Value Added Tax. The second is the combination of a wealth tax, taxing labor and capital at the same levels, and ending global tax avoidance schemes that allow multinational firms to avoid paying taxes (Saez and Zucman 2019). Saez and Zucman's tax proposal matters for housing because it targets the creation of excess capital at the disposal of elites that they shift from the primary to the secondary circuit of capital. Limiting excess capital takes the ammunition out of the hands of real estate speculators.

The progressive tax policies of an LVT, optimal tax rates on high earners, a wealth tax, and closing tax avoidance loopholes are good examples of social policy that signal a way out of the neoliberal project. However, it does not account for negative social or economic effects that stem from racism and racial segregation. As Massey and Denton (1993) showed, the historical effects of racial segregation limit the economic upturns and amplify the economic downturns for Black-owned businesses and property values in segregated neighborhoods. Racism in the labor market means less income and less generational wealth for African Americans. The neighborhood stigmas associated with predominantly Black neighborhoods acts as deterrent to capital investment. In other words, progressive taxation and curbing real estate speculation alone will not address the negative effects caused by racism. It would be different if the only barrier to a home or neighborhood was affordability. In fact, residential segregation is compatible with an LVT. Given the importance of white's racial preferences regarding housing, what happens when the most efficient use of allocating housing to minimize the economic impact of an LVT is to make housing racially segregated? Since the majority of whites have a preference for segregated neighborhoods, racially integrating buildings and neighborhoods triggers white flight. If the LVT is levied on underutilized land and empty housing units, then the economic incentive is to keep housing units racially segregated so as not to trigger white outmigration. Supply side approaches to the housing question need the filtering down process to work and work in a way where it is not housing abandoned by whites filtering down to Black families and homeowners. The cultural aspects of segregation, including social connections to mainstream society, the accumulation of cultural and social capital, also matter for a robust democratic society. Progressive taxation that targets the wealthy and elites will increase the amount of public capital generated from labor, but it is also important to have mandates regarding equal pay between white and Black workers, equal pay between men and women, and regulations as to how that capital is invested back into the poor and working-class communities. This includes financial reparations. In either situation, racism prevents any semblance of a rational housing system or redistribution system to form or function. Limitation notwithstanding, LVTs and progressive income and wealth taxes would go a long way to create a more just society.

The biggest obstacle to real affordable housing policy in America today is the persistence of the language of white-private/black-public. As Du Bois noted, the racial structures that formed in the era of international slavery continue to provide the negative meanings associated with blackness and positive meanings associated with whiteness. Racial languages concretize abstract racial structures. They take the meanings of whiteness and blackness to change the meanings of other concepts and social entities, like public and private, good and bad citizens, safe and dangerous neighborhoods, and rights. This is why racism is much more than a characteristic of individuals or an implicit bias or an ideology. It's an exercise of cultural power of elite whites as a group over ordinary white and Black Americans. Because racism is a social property of whites expressed through language, the study of racial inequality has to start with elite whites. America's housing question is rooted in the shifting meanings of white citizenship. A normative ideal of whiteness, what I've called white-private citizenship, underwrites the meaning of, and thus, shapes how whites value and have a preference for public and private entities. Whether we are talking about private or public, the real issue at stake is control—control over the state, its institutions, and the distribution of public capital. That is why even in the throes of American neoliberalism you can find well-financed public schools, senior housing, and much of the federal housing policy that socializes individual risk to encourage private homeownership in predominantly white neighborhoods. Whites generally lose their preference for public institutions when they perceive racial minorities benefiting from *their* tax dollars and when public places become too racially integrated for *their* tastes. I would calculate that the language of white-privatization becomes the dominant racial language in white communities when racial integration surpasses the 30% threshold. It would seem logical that when ordinary whites figure out that they no longer benefit from privatization they would abandon the project. Instead, many have doubled down on the idea of privatization and using markets to solve problems, as evidenced by Yes In My BackYard (YIMBYs), while others have retreated to ethnonationalist positions.

In order for America to answer its housing question, it must reclaim the value of public. It is time for the public sector to reenter the land market, not for the sake of ending an era of privately owned homes, but for the sake of establishing a public housing field that can increase the actual supply of affordable housing. To do that, the meaning of public has to be recast as a multiracial and multiethnic framework. Although urban regions remain racially segregated, they are still the actual sites and places where new meanings and forms of citizenship emerge. Urban citizenship grounded in a multiracial and ethnic framework targets the cultural and symbolic meanings that underwrite idealized citizenship. By displacing ascribed and legal statuses from the notion of good citizenship, it provides an opportunity to not only redefine the basis of inclusion and exclusion, but also the meaning of public. Housing is as good as any place to start. A new public housing field can establish racially and ethnically integrated urban spaces across urban regions. This requires a mandate that poverty and racial groupings be deconcentrated across urban regions. This institutionalizes the right to mobility for all rather than using portable housing policies, like vouchers, to concentrate poverty in racially segregated private housing markets. Situating affordable housing policy in a multiracial cultural framework is more than moving toward an equal distribution of collection consumption and resources. It's redefining housing as a right, a public good, and as a home. The key is ensuring that public and private housing fields are not racially segregated or exist as parallel fields. By tying the fate of whites and non-whites to a public field of affordable housing, it will make it more difficult for ordinary whites to devalue the public when there is an observable and direct benefit for whites. Multiracial means ensuring that whites also have a stake in and thus value the role of the public. Housing policy that excludes the white middle class on the basis that such policies are inefficient or that it leads to the overconsumption of affordable housing only reinforces language of white-private/black-public to devalue public and overvalue private entities. The key is to prevent equating the public with a stigma, which spoils the notion of public through relegating the public as something that cleans up after the private, something that is simply a safety net for those on the margins of economy, rather than as the foundation for the good life. This can only be done by deracializing American citizenship. And it has to start in America's urban areas.

NOTE

1. An article in medium by The NeoGeorgist does an excellent job reviewing Henry George's racism, especially his anti-Asian racism.

References

Aalbers, Manual B. 2016. *The Financialization of Housing: A Political Economy Approach*. New York: Routledge.

Alba, Richard and John Logan. 1991. "Variations on Two Themes: Racial and Ethnic Patterns in the Attainment of Suburban Residence." *Demography* 28: 431–453.

Alexander, Jefferey C. 2006. *The Civil Sphere*. New York: Oxford University Press.

Ambrosius, John D., John I. Gilderbloom, William J. Steele, Wesley L. Meares and Dennis Keating. 2015. "Forty Years of Rent Control: Reexamining New Jersey's Moderate Local Policies after the Great Recession." *Cities* 49: 121–133.

Americans for Financial Reform. 2020. "Fact Sheet: Private Equity Vultures Eye Real Estate During Coronavirus Crisis." Americans for Financial Reform. Accessed July 8, 2021. https://ourfinancialsecurity.org/2020/04/fact-sheet-private-equity-vultures-eye-real-estate-during-coronavirus-crisis/.

Anderson, Benedict. 2016. *Imagined Communities: Reflections on the Origins and Spread of Nationalism*. New York: Verso.

Arias, Melanie Kayser Schmidt. 2013. *Experimental Citizens: The Experimental Housing Allowance Program and Housing Vouchers as American Social Policy in the 1970s and 1980s*. PhD diss. Los Angeles, CA: University of California.

Asquith, Brian J., Evan Mast and Davin Reed. 2021. "Local Effects of Large New Apartment Buildings in Low-Income Areas." *The Review of Economics and Statistics* 1–46.

Austin, Curtis J. and Elbert "Big Man" Howard. 2006. *Up Against the Wall: Violence in the Making and Unmaking of the Black Panther Party*. Fayetteville, AR: University of Arkansas Press.

Autor, David, Christopher J. Palmer and Parag A. Pathak. 2014. "Housing Market Spillovers: Evidence from the End of Rent Control in Cambridge, Massachusetts." *Journal of Political Economy* 122(3): 661–717.

Ball, Michael. 1994. "The 1980s Property Boom." *Environment and Planning* A 26: 671–695.

Baranski, John. 2009. "Something to Help Themselves: Tenant Organizing in San Francisco's Public Housing, 1965–1975." *Journal of Urban History* 33(3): 418–442.

Barkey, Karen. 2011. "Historical Sociology." In *The Oxford Handbook of Analytical Sociology*, edited by Peter Bearman and Peter Hedstrom, 712–734. Oxford: Oxford University Press.

Barton, Stephen E. 1985. "The Neighborhood Movement in San Francisco." *Berkeley Planning Journal* 2(1): 85–104.

Barton, Stephen E. 2011. "The City's Wealth and the City's Limits: Progressive Housing Policy in Berkeley, California, 1976–2011." *Journal of Planning History* 11(2): 160–178.

Bauman, Zygmunt. 1998. *Globalization: The Human Consequences*. Cambridge: Polity Press

Bayliss, Kate. 2014. "The Financialization of Water." *Review of Radical Political Economics* 46(3): 292–307.

Beckert, Sven. 2015. *Empire of Cotton: A Global History*. New York: Vintage Books.

Bell, Alison, Barbara Sard and Becky Koepnick. 2018. "Prohibiting Housing Discrimination Against Renter with Vouchers Improves Results: Lessons From Cities and States that have Enacted Source Income Laws." *Center on Budget and Policy Priorities* 1–21.

Bell Jr., Derrick A. 1980. "Brown v. Board of Education and the Interest-Convergence Dilemma." *Harvard Law Review* 518: 518–533.

Bell, Derrick Bell. 1987. *And We Are Not Saved: The Elusive Quest for Racial Justice*. New York: Basic Books.

Berk, Gerald and Marc Schneiberg. 2005. "Varieties in Capitalism, Varieties of Association: Collaborative Learning in American Industry, 1900–1925." *Politics and Society* 33(1): 46–87.

Beyon, Erdmann Doane. 1938. "The Voodoo Cult Among Negro Migrants to Detroit." *American Journal of Sociology* 43(6): 894–907.

Bier, Thomas. 2001. "Moving Up, Filtering Down: Metropolitan Housing Dynamics and Public Policy." The Brookings Institution Center on Urban and Metropolitan Policy.

Binkovitz, Leah. 2019. "Gap Between Income Growth and Housing Cost Increases Continues to Grow." Rice Kinder Institute for Urban Research. Accessed July 8, 2021. https://kinder.rice.edu/urbanedge/2019/07/25/gap-between-income-growth-and-housing-cost-increases-continues-grow.

Bloom, Nicolas Dagen. 2009. *Public Housing That Worked: New York in the Twentieth Century*. Philadelphia, PA: University of Pennsylvania Press.

Bluementhal, Pamela, John R. McGinty and Rolf Pendall. 2016. "Strategies for Increasing Hosuing Supply in High-Cost Cities." Washington, DC: The Urban Institute.

Bonilla-Silva, Eduardo. 1996. "Rethinking Racism: Toward a Structural Interpretation." *American Sociological Review* 64: 465–480.

Bonilla-Silva, Eduardo. 2017. *Racism without Racists: Color-Blind Racism and the Persistence of Racial Inequality in America*, 5th edition. Lanham, MD: Rowman & Littlefield.

Bonneval, L. and F. Roberts, 2013. *L'immeuble de Rapport. L'immobilier Entre Gestion et Spéculation: Lyon, 1860-1990*. Rennes Presses: Universitaires de Rennes.

Bourdieu, Pierre. 1990. *The Logic of Practice*. Stanford, CA: Stanford University Press.

Braudel ([1945] 1995). *The Mediterranean and the Mediterranean World in the Age of Philip II*. Los Angeles, CA: University of California Press.

Brown, Greg and Hunter Glanz. 2018. "Identifying Potential NIMBY and YIMBY Effects in General Land Use Planning and Zoning." *Applied Geography* 99: 1–11.

Brown-Saracino, Japonica. 2009. *A Neighborhood That Never Changes: Gentrification, Social Preservation, and the Search for Authenticity*. Chicago, IL: University of Chicago Press.

Brubaker, Rogers. 1992. *Citizenship and Nationhood in France and Germany*. Cambridge: Harvard University Press.

Bruce, Susannah. 2016. "Pursuing Urban Commons: Politics and Alliances in Community Land Trust Activism in East London" *Antipode* 48(1): 134–150.

Calhoun, Michael. 2018. "Lessons From The Financial Crisis: The Central Importance of a Sustainable, Affordable, and Inclusive Housing Market" Brookings. Accessed July 8, 2021. https://www.brookings.edu/research/lessons-from-the-financial-crisis-the-central-importance-of-a-sustainable-affordable-and-inclusive-housing-market/.

Campbell, John L. and Ove K. Pedersen. 2014. *The National Origins of Policy Ideas: Knowledge Regimes in the United States, France, Germany, and Denmark*. Princeton, NJ: Princeton University Press.

Castells, Manuel. 1983. *The City and the Grassroots: A Cross Cultural Theory of Urban Social Movements*. Berkeley, CA: University of California Press.

Castells, Manuel. 2011. *The Information Age: Economy, Society, and Culture Volume 1: The Rise of the Network Society*, 2nd edition. New York: Wiley and Blackwell.

Chun, Edna and Joe Feagin. 2020. *Rethinking Diversity Frameworks in Higher Education*. New York: Routledge.

Clay, Phillip. 1979. "The Process of Black Suburbanization." *Urban Affairs Quarterly* 14(4): 405–424.

Coggin, Thomas and Marius Pieterse. 2015. "A Right to Transport? Moving Towards a Rights Based Approach to Mobility in the City." *South African Journal on Human Rights* 31(2): 294–314.

Collins, William J. and Robert A. Margo. 2011. "Race and Home Ownership from the End of the Civil War to the Present." *The American Economic Review* 101(3): 355–359.

Cook-Martin, David. 2013. *The Scramble for Citizens: Dual Nationality and State Competition for Immigrants*. Stanford, CA: Stanford University Press.

Copeland, Roy W. 2013. "In the Beginning: Origins of African American Real Property Ownership in the United States." *Journal of Black Studies* 44(6): 646–664.

Cottom, Tressie McMillan. 2017. *Lower Ed: The Troubling Rise of For Profit Colleges in the New Economy*. New York: The New Press.

Crenshaw, Kimberle. 1989. "Demarginalizing the Intersection of Race and Sex: A Black Feminist Critique of Antidiscrimination Doctrine, Feminist Theory and Antiracist Policies." *University of Chicago Legal Forum* 1: 139–167.

Cresswell, Tim. 2006. "The Right to Mobility: The Production of Mobility in the Courtroom." *Antipode* 38(4): 735–754.

Cresswell, Tim. 2010. "Toward a Politics of Mobility." *Environment and Planning D: Society and Space* 28: 17–31.

Cresswell, Tim. 2013. "Citizenship in the Worlds of Mobility." In *Critical Mobilities*, edited by O. Soderstrom, S. Randeria, and G. D'Amato, 105–124. New York: Routledge.

Davis, John Emmeus. 2010. "Origins and Evolution of the Common Land Trust in the United States." In *The Community Land Trust Reader*, edited by John Emmeus Davis, 3–47. Cambridge, MA: Lincoln Institute of Land Policy.

Davis, Mike. 1990. *City of Quartz: Excavating the Future in Los Angeles*. New York: Verso.

Delgado, Richard and Jean Stefancic. 2001. *Critical Race Theory: An Introduction*. New York: NYU Press.

Desmond, Mathew. 2017. *Evicted: Poverty and Profit in the American City*. New York: Penguin Random House.

Diamond, Rebecca, Tim McQuade and Franklin Qian. 2018. "The Effect of Rent Control Expansion on Tenants, Landlords, and Inequality: Evidence from San Francisco." National Bureau of Economic Research Working Paper no. 24181.

DiMaggio, Paul (ed). 1991. *The New Institutionalism in Organizational Analysis*. Chicago, IL: Chicago University Press.

Domhoff, William and Richard Gendron. 2009. *The Leftmost City; Power and Progressive Politics in Santa Cruz*. Boulder, CO: Westview Press.

Doti, Lynne P. 2016. *Financing California Real Estate: Spanish Missions to Subprime Real Estate*. New York: Routledge.

Dougherty, Conor. 2020. *Golden Gates: The Housing Crisis and a Reckoning for the American Dream*. New York: Penguin Press.

Du Bois, W. E. B. 1995. *The Souls of Black Folk*. New York: Penguin Books.

Du Bois, W. E. B. 1969. "The Souls of White Folk." In *Darkwater: Voices from within the Veil,* 29–52. New York: Shocken Books.

Dubois, W. E. B. 1899. *The Philadelphia Negro*. Philadelphia, PA: University of Pennsylvania Press.

Ellen, Ingrid and Brendan O'Flaherty. 2013. "How New York Housing Policies Are Different—and Maybe Why." In *New York City-Los Angeles: The Uncertain Future*, edited by A. Beveridge, & D. Halle. Oxford: Oxford University Press.

Faber, Jacob W. 2020. "We Built This: Consequences of New Deal Era Intervention in America's Racial Geography." *American Sociological Review* 85(5): 739–775.

Feagin, Joe. 2006. *Systemic Racism: A Theory of Oppression*. New York: Routledge.

Feagin, Joe. 2013. *The White Racial Frame: Centuries of Racial Framing and Counter-Framing*. New York: Routledge.

Feagin, Joe and Kimberly Ducey. 2018. *Racist America: Roots, Current Realities, and Future Reparations*. New York: Routledge.

Federal Deposit Insurance Corporation. 1997. "History of the Eighties, Lessons for the Future, Volume I: An Examination of the Banking Crises of the 1980s and Early 1990s." Washington, DC. https://www.fdic.gov/bank/historical/history/vol1.html.

Federal Reserve Bank of St. Louis. 2019. S&P/Case Shiller US National Home Price Index. https://fred.stlouisfed.org/series/CSUSHPISA.

Fields, Desiree. 2015. "Contesting the Financialization of Urban Space: Community Organizations and the Struggle to Preserve Affordable Rental Housing in New York City." *Journal of Urban Affairs* 37(2): 144–165.

Fields, Desiree and Sabina Uffer. 2016. "The Financialisation of Rental Housing: A Comparative Analysis of New York City and Berlin." *Urban Studies* 53(7): 1486–1502.

Fligstein, Neil. 2001. *The Architecture of Markets: An Economic Sociology of 21st Capitalist Societies.* Princeton, NJ: Princeton University Press.

Fligstein, Neil and Doug McAdam. 2011. "Toward a General Theory of Strategic Action Fields." *Sociological Theory* 29(1): 1–26.

Fligstein, Neil and Doug McAdam. 2012. *A Theory of Fields.* Oxford: Oxford University Press.

Fligstein, Neil and Jacob Habinek. 2014. "Sucker Punched by the Invisible Hand: The World Financial Markets and the Globalization of the US Mortgage Crisis." *Socio-Economic Review* 1–29.

Florida, Richard. 2002. *The Rise of the Creative Class and How it's Transforming Work, Leisure and Everyday Life.* New York: Basic Books.

Fraser, Nancy. 1994."After The Family Wage: Gender Equity and the Welfare State." *Political Theory* 22(4): 591–618.

Freund, David. 2010. *Colored Property: State Policy & White Racial Politics in Suburban America.* Chicago, IL: University of Chicago Press.

Frey, William H. 2001. *"Melting Pot Suburbs: A Census 2000 Study of Suburban Diversity."* Washington, DC: Brookings Institution.

Frey, William H. 2011. *"Melting Pot Cities and Suburbs: Racial and Ethnic Change in Metro America in the 2000s."* Washington, DC: Brookings Institution.

Friedman, Milton. 1975. *There is No Such Thing as a Free Lunch: Essays on Public Policy.* New York: Open Court Publishing.

Furman Center. 2017. "2017 Focus: Changes in New York City's Housing Stock." The State of New York City's Housing and Neighborhood Report. Accessed July 8, 2021. https://furmancenter.org/files/sotc/SOC_2017_FOCUS_Changes_in_NYC _Housing_Stock_1JUN2018.pdf.

Garrow, David. 1986. *Bearing the Cross: Martin Luther King Jr., and the Southern Christian Leadership Conference.* New York: Quill.

Gates, Conor. 2020. *Golden Gates: Fighting for Housing in America.* New York: Penguin Press.

George, Henry. [1879] 2009. *Progress and Poverty.* New York: Dodo Press.

Ghaziani, Amin. 2014. *There Goes the Gayborhood?* Princeton, NJ: Princeton University Press.

Ghaziani, Amin. 2019. "Cultural Archipelagos: New Directions in the Study of Sexuality and Space." *City and Community* 18(1): 4–22.

Gilderbloom, John I. and Richard Applebaum. 1987. "Toward a Sociology of Rent: Are Rental Housing Markets Competitive?" *Social Problems* 34(3) 261–276.

Gilderbloom, John and Lin Ye. 2007. "Thirty Years of Rent Control: A Survey of New Jersey Cities." *Journal of Urban Affairs* 29: 207–220.

Gilens, Martin. 1999. *Why Americans Hate Welfare: Race, Media, and the Politics of Antipoverty Policy*. Chicago, IL: University of Chicago Press.

Glaeser Edward L. 2019. "The Macroeconomic Implications of Housing Supply Restrictions." In *Hot Property: Housing Markets in Major Cities*, edited by Rob Nijskens, Melanie Lohuis, Paul Hilbers, Willem Heeringa, 99–108. Springer.

Glaeser, Edward and Brye A. Ward, 2009. "The Causes and Consequences of Land Use Regulation: Evidence from Greater Boston." *Journal of Urban Economics* 65: 265–278.

Glaeser, Edward L., Joseph Gyourko, and Raven Saks. 2005. "Why Is Manhattan So Expensive? Regulation and the Rise of Housing Prices." *Journal of Law and Economics* 48: 331–369.

Glaeser, Edward L. and Joseph Gyourko. 2005. "Urban Decline and Durable Housing." *Journal of Political Economy* 113(2): 345–375.

Glaeser, Edward L. and Joseph Gyourko. 2018. "The Economic Implications of Housing Supply." *Journal of Economic Perspectives* 32(1): 3–30.

Glaeser, Edward L., Joseph Gyourko and Albert Saiz. 2008. "Housing Supply and Housing Bubbles." *Journal of Urban Economics* 64(2): 198–217.

Goldstein, Adam. 2018. "The Social Ecology of Speculation and Non-Occupancy Investment in the US Housing Bubble." *American Sociological Review* 83(6): 1108–1143.

Gotham, Kevin Fox. 2006. "The Secondary Circuit of Capital Reconsidered: Globalization and the US Real Estate Sector." *American Journal of Sociology* 112(1): 231–275.

Gottdiener, Mark, Randolph Hohle and Colby King. 2019. *The New Urban Sociology*, 6th edition. Routledge: New York

Gottdiener, Mark. 1977. *Planned Sprawl: Public and Private Interest in Suburbia*. Beverley Hills: Sage Press.

Gottdiener, Mark. 1994. *The Social Reproduction of Urban Space*, 2nd edition. Austin, TX: University of Texas Press

Green, Richard, Stephen Malpezzi and Stephen K. Mayo. 2005. "Metropolitan-Specific Estimates of the Price Elasticity of Supply of Housing, and Their Sources." *American Economic Review* 95(2): 334–339.

Grossman, Mark. 1975. "The New York City Housing Receivership and Community Management Programs." *Fordham Urban Law Journal* 3(8): 637–660.

Gyourko, Joseph and Peter Linneman. 1989. "Equity and Efficiency Aspects of Rent Control: An Empirical Study of New York City." *Journal of Urban Economics* 26: 54–74.

Gyourko, Joseph, Christopher Mayer and Todd Sinai. 2013. "Superstar Cities." *American Economic Journal - Economic Policy* 5(4): 167–199.

Hackworth, Jason. 2019. *Manufacturing Decline: How Racism and The Conservative Movement Crush the American Rust Belt*. New York: Columbia University Press.

Hague, Euan. 2010. "The Right to Enter Every Other State – The Supreme Court and African American Mobility in the United States." *Mobilities* 5: 331–347.

Harris, Richard. 2012. "'Ragged Urchins Play on Marquetry Floors': The Discourse of Filtering is Reconstructed, 1920s–1950s." *Housing Policy Debate* 22(3): 463–482.

Harris, Richard. 2013. "The Rise of Filtering Down: The American Housing Market Transformed, 1915–1929." *Social Science History* 37(4): 515–549.

Harvey, David. 1973. *Social Justice and the City.* Baltimore, MD: John Hopkins University Press.

Harvey, David. 1978. "The Urban Process under Capitalism: A Framework for Analysis." *International Journal of Urban and Regional Research* 2: 101–131.

Harvey, David. 2012. *Rebel Cities: From the Right to the City to the Urban Revolution.* New York: Verso.

Haughwout, Andrew, Richard Peach, John Spoon and Joesph Tracey. 2012. "The Supply Side of the Housing Boom and Bust of the 2000s." Federal Reserve Bank of New York.

Healy, Kieran. 2006. *Last Best Gifts: Altruism and the Market for Human Blood and Organs.* Chicago, IL: University of Chicago Press.

Hendricks, Kasey and Dania Cheyenne Harvey. 2017. "Not One But Many: Monetary Punishment and The Fergusons of America." *Sociological Forum* 32(1): 930–951.

Hertz, Susan Handley. 1981. *The Welfare Mothers' Movement: A Decade of Change for Poor Women?* Washington DC: University Press in America.

Hillard, David (ed). 2008. *The Black Panther Party: Service to the People Programs.* University of Albuquerque, NM: New Mexico Press.

Hirsch, Arnold. 1983. *Making the Second Ghetto: Race and Housing in Chicago 1940–1960.* Chicago, IL: University of Chicago Press.

Hohle, Randolph. 2009a. "The Body and Citizenship in Social Movement Research: Embodied Performances and the Deracialized Self in the Black Civil Rights Movement 1961–1965." *The Sociological Quarterly* 50(2): 283–307.

Hohle, Randolph. 2009b. "The Rise of the New South Governmentality: Competing Southern Revitalization Projects and Police Responses to the Black Civil Rights Movement 1961–1965." *Journal of Historical Sociology* 22(4): 497–527.

Hohle, Randolph. 2012. "The Color of Neoliberalism: The 'Modern Southern Businessman' and Post-War Alabama's Challenge to Racial Desegregation." *Sociological Forum* 27(1): 142–162.

Hohle, Randolph. 2013. *Black Citizenship and Authenticity in the Civil Rights Movement.* New York: Routledge.

Hohle, Randolph. 2015. *Race and the Origins of American Neoliberalism.* New York: Routledge.

Hohle, Randolph. 2018. *Racism in the Neoliberal Era: A Meta History of Elite White Power.* New York: Routledge.

Hohle, Randolph. 2021. "Unruly Bodies: Figurate Violence and the State's Responses to the Black Panther Party." In *The Oxford Handbook of the Sociology of Body and Embodiment.* Oxford: Oxford University Press

Holston, Jason. 2001. "Urban Citizenship and Globalization." In *Global City-Regions: Trends, Theory, Policy*, edited by Allen J. Scott, 325–348. Oxford: Oxford University Press.

Howell Junia and Elizabeth Korver-Glenn. 2018. "Neighborhoods, Race, and the Twenty-first century Housing Appraisal Industry." *Sociology of Race and Ethnicity* 4(4): 473–490.

Howlett, Michael and Ben Cashore. 2009. "The Dependent Variable Problem in the Study of Policy Change: Understanding Policy Change as a Methodological Problem." *Journal of Contemporary Policy Analysis* 11(1): 29–42.

Husock, Howard. 2019. "Public Housing Becomes the Latest Progressive Fantasy." *The Atlantic*. https://www.theatlantic.com/ideas/archive/2019/11/public-housing-fundamentally-flawed/602515/.

Hyra, Derek. 2012. "Conceptualizing the New Urban Renewal: Comparing the Past to the Present." *Urban Affairs Review* 48(4): 498–527.

Hyra, Derek. 2017. *Race, Class, and Politics in the Cappuccino City*. Chicago, IL: University of Chicago Press.

Ip, Greg and Mark Whitehouse. 2006. "How Milton Friedman Changed Economics, Policy and Markets." The Wall Street Journal Online 17.

Jackson, Mandi Isaacs. 2006. "Harlem's Rent Strike and Rat War: Representation, Housing Access and Tenant Resistance in New York, 1958–1964." *American Studies* 47(1): 53–79.

Joint Center for Housing Studies of Harvard University. 2018. T*he State of the Nation's Housing*. Harvard University.

Kantor, Paul. 2013. "The Two Faces of American Urban Policy." *Urban Affairs Review* 49(6): 821–850.

Katz, Alisa Belinkoff, Peter Chesney and Lindsay Alissa King. 2018. "People are Simply Unable to Pay the Rent": What History Tells Us About Rent Control in Los Angeles." UCLA Luskin Center for History and Policy.

Keating, W. Dennis. 1983. "Rent Control in California: Responding to the Housing Crisis." Institute of Government Studies, California Agencies. Paper 410.

Kelly Jr., James J. 2015. "Sustaining Neighborhoods of Choice: From Landbank(ing) to Landtrust(ing)." *Washington Law Journal* 3(54.)

Knuth, Sarah. 2018. "Breakthroughs" for a Green Economy? Financialization and Clean Energy Transition." *Energy Research & Social Science* 41: 220–229.

Korver-Glenn, Elizabeth. 2018. "Compounding Inequalities: How Racial Stereotypes and Discrimination Accumulate across the Stages of Housing Exchange." *American Sociological Review* 83(4): 627–656.

Kruse, Kevin. 2005. *White Flight: Atlanta and the Making of Modern Conservatism*. Princeton, NJ: Princeton University Press.

Krysan, Maria and Kyle Crowder. 2017. *Cycle of Segregation: Social Processes and Residential Segregation*. New York: Sage.

Krzewinski, Lisa M. 2001. "Section 8's Failure to Integrate: The Interaction of Class Based and Racial Discrimination." *Boston College Third World Law Journal* Issue 2: 315.

Kymlicka, Will. 1995. *Multicultural Citizenship: A Liberal Theory of Minority Rights*. Oxford: Oxford University Press.

Lachmann, Richard. 2002. *Capitalists in Spite of Themselves: Elite Conflict and Economic Transitions in Early Modern Europe*. Oxford: Oxford University Press.

Lachmann, Richard. 2013. *What is Historical Sociology*. Cambridge: Polity Press.

Lands, LeeAnn. 2008. "Be a Patriot, Buy a Home: Re-Imagining Home Owners and Home Ownership in Early 20th Century Atlanta." *Journal of Social History* 41(4): 943–965.

Lateef, Husain and David Androff. 2017. "Children Can't Learn on an Empty Stomach": The Black Panther Party's Free Breakfast Program." *Journal of Sociology & Social Welfare* 44(4): 3–17.

Lees, Loretta, Hyun Bang Shin, Ernesto Lopez-Morales. 2016. *Planetary Gentrification*. New York: Wiley.

Lefebvre, Henri. 1991. *The Production of Space*. Oxford: Blackwell.

Lefebvre, Henri. 1996. "Right to the City." In *Writing on Cities*, edited by Kofman and E. Lebas, 147–159. New York: Blackwell.

Leighninger, Jr., Robert. 2007. *Long-Range Public Investment: The Forgotten Legacy of the New Deal*. Columbia, SC: University of South Carolina Press.

Levin, Eric J. and Gwilym B. J. Pryce. 2009. "What Determines the Price Elasticity of House Supply? Real Interest Rate Effects and Cyclical Asymmetries." *Housing Studies* 24(6): 713–736.

Lister, Ruth. 1997. *Citizenship: Feminist Perspectives*. New York: MacMillian.

Lincoln, C. Eric. 1961. *The Black Muslims in America*. Boston, MA: Beacon Press.

Logan, John and Harvey Molotch. 1987. *Urban Fortunes: The Political Economy of Place*. Berkeley, CA: University of California Press.

Logan, John R. 2014. "Separate and Unequal in Suburbia." Census Brief prepared for Project US2010.

Logan, John R. and Richard D. Alba. 1995. "Who Lives in Affluent Suburbs? Racial Differences in Eleven Metropolitan Regions." *Sociological Focus* 28: 353–364.

Maney, Brian and Sheila Crowley. 2000. "Scarcity and Success: Perspectives on Assisted Housing." *Journal of Affordable Housing and Community Development Law* 9(4): 319–368.

March, James G. and Johan P. Olsen. 1984. "The New Institutionalism: Organizational Factors in Political Life." *The American Political Science Review* 78(3): 734–774.

March, James G. and Johan P. Olsen. 2011. "Elaborating the "New Institutionalism." In *The Oxford Handbook of Political Science,* edited by Sarah A. Binder, R. A. W. Rhodes, and Bert A. Rockman. Oxford: Oxford University Press.

Marcuse, Peter. [1978] 2016. "The Myths of Housing Policy." In *In Defense of Housing: The Politics of Crisis*, edited by D. Madden and P. Marcuse, 119–144. New York: Verso.

Mari, Fransesca. 2020. "A $60 Billion Housing Grab by Wall Street" The New York Times Magazine. https://www.nytimes.com/2020/03/04/magazine/wall-street-landlords.html.

Marshal, Thomas Humphrey. 1964. *Class, Citizenship, and Social Development: Essays*. New York: Doubleday.

Martin, Isaac. 2008. *The Permanent Tax Revolt: How The Property Tax Transformed American Politics*. Stanford, CA: Stanford University Press.

Mason, J. W. 2019. "Considerations on Rent Control" jwmason.org. https://jwmason.org/slackwire/considerations-on-rent-control/.

Massey, Douglas and Jonathan Tannen 2015. "A Research Note on Trends in Black Hypersegregation." *Demography* 52(3): 1025–1034.

Massey, Douglas and Nancy Denton. 1993. *American Apartheid: Segregation and the Making of the Underclass*. Cambridge, MA: Harvard University Press.

Mast, Evan. 2019, "The Effect of New Market Rate Housing Construction on the Low-Income Housing Market." Upjohn Working Papers and Journal Articles 19-307, W.E. John Institute, Employment Research.

Mathews, Zoie. 2019. "You've Heard of NIMBYs – but Who Are the PHIMBYs?" Los Angeles Magazine. https://www.lamag.com/citythinkblog/who-are-the-phimbys/.

McAdam, Doug. 1996. "The Framing Function of Movement Tactics: Strategy Dramaturgy in the American Civil Rights Movement." In *Comparative Perspectives on Social Movements,* edited by Doug McAdam, John McCarthy, and Mayer Zald, 338–355. Cambridge: Cambridge University Press.

McCabe, Brian J. 2016. *No Place Like Home: Wealth, Community and the Politics of Homeownership*. Oxford: Oxford University Press.

McElroy, Erin and Andrew Szeto. 2017. "The Racial Contours of YIMBY/NIMBY Bay Area Gentrification." *Berkeley Planning Journal* 29(1): 7–45.

McKenna, William. 1982. *The Report of The Presidents Commission on Housing*. Washington, DC.

Mears, Ashley. 2011. *Pricing Beauty: The Making of a Fashion Model*. Berkeley, CA: University of California Press.

Meehan, James. 2014. "Reinventing Real Estate: The Community Land Trust as a Social Invention in Affordable Housing." *Journal of Applied Social Science* 8(2): 113–133.

Meier, August and Elliot Rudwick. 1975. *CORE: A Study in the Civil Rights Movement, 1942 1968*. Urbana, IL: University of Illinois Press.

Mele, Christopher. 2000. *Selling the Lower East Side: Culture, Real Estate, and Resistance in New York City*. Minneapolis, MN: University of Minnesota Press.

Mende Samstein Papers. "Some Proposals for a Housing Campaign" Box 1 Folder 1, Wisconsin Historical Archives, Madison Wisconsin.

Meyer, Stephen Grant. 2000. *As Long As They Don't Move Next Door: Segregation and Racial Conflict in American Neighborhoods*. New York: Rowman and Littlefield.

Miriam Zuk and Karen Chapple. 2016. "Housing Production, Filtering and Displacement: Untangling the Relationships." Research Brief. Institute of Governmental Studies, University of California at Berkeley.

Mollenkopf, J. 1975. "The Postwar Politics of Urban Development." *Politics and Society* 5: 247–296.

Monkkonen, Eric H. 1988. *America Becomes Urban: The Development of US Cities and Towns 1780-1980*. Berkeley, CA: University of California Press.

Moran, Dominique, Nick Gill, and Deirdre Conlon. 2013 (ed). *Carceral Spaces: Mobility and Agency in Imprisonment and Migrant Detention*. London: Ashgate.

Nelson, Alondra. 2011. *Body and Soul: The Black Panther Party and the Fight Against Medical Discrimination*. Minneapolis, MN: University of Minnesota Press.

Neuman, Tracey. 2016. *Remaking the Rust Belt: The Post-Industrial Transformation of North America*. Philadelphia, PA: University of Pennsylvania Press.

New York State Division of Housing and Community Renewal. 1993. "Rent Regulation After 50 Years: An Overview of New York State's Rent Regulated Housing."

Nguyen, Mai Thi, Victoria Basolo and Abhishek Tiwari. 2013. "Opposition to Affordable Housing in the USA: Debate Framing and Responses of Local Actors." *Housing, Theory, and Society* 30(2): 107–130.

Oakley, Deidre and Hui-Shen Tsao. 2007. "Socioeconomic Gains and Spillover Effects of Geographically Targeted Initiatives to Combat Economic Distress: An Examination of Chicago's Empowerment Zone." *Cities* 24(1): 43–59.

Oakley, Deidre, J. Fraser and J. Bazain. 2015. "The Imagine and Self-Sufficient Communities of HOPE VI: Examining the Community and Social Support Component." *Urban Affairs Review* 51(5): 726–746.

Park, Robert E., Ernest Burgess and Roderick McKenzie. 1925. *The City*. Chicago, IL: University of Chicago Press.

Pattillo, Mary. 2013. "Housing: Commodity versus Right." *Annual Review of Sociology* 39: 509–31.

Pattillo-McCoy, Mary. 1999. *Black Picket Fences: Privilege and Peril among the Black Middle Class*. Chicago, IL: University of Chicago Press.

Pendergrast, Mark. 2017. *City on the Verge: Atlanta and the Fight for America's Future*. New York: Basic Books.

Perez, Miguel. 2017. "Reframing Housing Strategies." *City* 21(5): 530–549.

Phillips, Shane. 2020. *The Affordable City: Strategies for Putting Housing Within Reach (and Keeping it There)*. New York: Island Press.

Piketty, Thomas, Emmanuel Saez, and Stefanie Stantcheva. 2014. "Optimal Taxation of Top Labor Incomes: A Tale of Three Elasticities." *American Economic Journal: Economic Policy* 6(1): 230–271.

Public Accountability Initiative. 2019. *Real Estate's Outsized Influence Over New York State Rent Laws*. Special Report, June.

Purcell, Mark. 1997. "Ruling Los Angeles: Neighborhood Movements, Urban Regimes, and the Production of Space in Southern California." *Urban Geography* 18(8): 684–704.

Purcell, Mark. 2002. "Excavating Lefebvre: The Right to the City and its Urban Politics of the Inhabitant." *GeoJournal* 58: 99–108.

Purcell, Mark. 2003. "Citizenship and the Right to the Global City: Reimagining the Capitalist World Order." *International Journal of Urban and Regional Research* 27: 564–590.

Purcell, Mark. 2013. "Possible Worlds: Henri Lefebvre and the Right to the City." *Journal of Urban Affairs* 36(1): 141–154.

Quadagno, Jill. 1994. *The Color of Welfare: How Racism Undermined the War on Poverty.* New York: Oxford University Press.

Quinn, William and John D. Turner. 2020. *Boom and Bust: A Global History of Financial Bubbles.* Cambridge University Press.

Radford, G. 1992. "New Building and Investment Patterns in 1920s Chicago." *Social Science History* 16(1): 1–21.

Radford, G. 1996. *Modern Housing for America: Policy Struggles in the New Deal Era.* Chicago, IL: University of Chicago Press.

Raetz, Hayley, Elizabeth Kneebone and Carolina Reid. 20202. "The Hard Costs of Construction: Recent Trends in Labor and Materials Costs for Apartment Buildings in California." A Terner Center Report. Terner Center for Housing Innovation, University of California at Berkeley.

Ralph, Jr. James R. 1993. *Northern Protest: Martin Luther King, Jr., Chicago, and the Civil Rights Movement.* Cambridge: Harvard University Press.

Ratcliff, Richard U. 1945. "Filtering down and the Elimination of Substandard Housing." *The Journal of Land & Public Utility Economics* 21(4): 322–330.

Retsinas, Nicolas R. and Eric Belsky (ed). 2008. R*evisiting Rental Housing: Policies, Programs, and Priorities.* Washington, DC: Brookings Institution Press.

Rhomberg, Chris. 2004. *No There There: Race, Class, and Political Community in Oakland.* Berkeley, CA: University of California Press.

Roberson, D. and D. Judd 1989. *The Development of American Public Policy: The Structure of Policy Restraint.* Glenview, IL. Scott Foresman.

Roediger, David R. 2018. *Working Towards Whiteness: How America's Immigrants Became White. The Strange Journey from Ellis Island to the Suburbs. Updated Edition.* New York: Basic Books.

Roger Freidland. 1982. *Power and Crisis in the City.* London: MacMillan.

Roscigno, Vincent J., Diana L. Karafin and Griff Tester. 2009. "The Complexities and Processes of Racial Housing Discrimination." *Social Problems* 56(1): 49–69.

Rosen, Eva. 2020. *The Voucher Promise: "Section 8" and the Fate of an American Neighborhood.* Princeton, NJ: Princeton University Press.

Rosenthal, Stuart S. 2014. "Are Private Markets and Filtering a Viable Source of Low-Income Housing? Estimates from a 'Repeat Income' Model." *The American Economic Review* 104(2): 687–706.

Ross, Catherine E., John R. Reynolds and Karlyn J. Geis. 2000. "The Contingent Meaning of Neighborhood Stability for Residents' Psychological Well-Being." *American Sociological Review* 65(4): 581–597.

Rothstein, Richard. 2017. *The Color of Law: A Forgotten History of How Our Government Segregated America.* New York: Liverlight.

Rubinwitz, Leonard and James Rosenaum. 2000. *Crossing the Class and Color Lines: From Public Housing to White Suburbia.* Chicago, IL: University of Chicago Press.

Rugh, Jacob S. and Douglas S. Massey. 2010. "Racial Segregation and the American Foreclosure Crisis." *American Sociological Review* 75(5): 629–651.

Sabatier, Paul and Hank Jenkins-Smith. 1993. *Policy Learning and Policy Change: An Advocacy Coalition Approach.* Boulder, CO: Westview Press.

Saez, Emmanuel and Gabriel Zucman. 2019. *The Triumph of Injustice: How the Rich Dodge Taxes and How to Make them Pay*. New York: Norton.

Safford, Sean. 2009. *Why the Garden Club Couldn't Save Youngstown: The Transformation of the Rust Belt*. Cambridge: Harvard University Press.

Sard, Barbara, Douglas Rice, Alison Bell and Alicia Mazzara. 2018. "Federal Policy Changes Can Help More Families with Housing Vouchers Live in Higher-Opportunity Areas." *Center on Budget and Policy Priorities* 1–30.

Sassen, Saskia. 1988. *The Mobility of Labor and Capital: A Study in International Investment and Labor Flow*. Cambridge: Cambridge University Press.

Sassen, Saskia. 1991. *The Global City: New York, London, Toyko*. Princeton, NJ: Princeton University Press.

Schively, Carissa. 2007. "Understanding the NIMBY and LULU Phenomena: Reassessing Our Knowledge Base and Informing Future Research." *Journal of Planning Literature* 21(3): 255–266.

Schneiberg, Marc. 2013. "Movements as Political Conditions for Diffusion: Anti-corporatist Movements and the Spread of Cooperative Forms in American Capitalism." *Organizational Studies* 34(5–6): 653–682.

Schneiberg, Marc and Tim Bartley. 2008. "Organizations, Regulations, and Economic Behavior: Regulatory Dynamics and Forms from the Nineteenth to Twenty-First Century." *Annual Review of Law and Social Science* 4: 31–61.

Schneider, Mark and John R. Logan. 1982. "Suburban Racial Segregation and Black Access to Local Public Resources." *Social Science Quarterly* 63: 762–770.

Schwartz, Joel. 1983. "The New York City Rent Strikes of 1963-1964." *Social Service Review* 57(4): 545–564.

Sears, David and Jack Citron. 1982. *The Tax Revolt: Something for Nothing in California*. Cambridge: Harvard University Press.

Seidman, Steven. 2002. *Beyond the Closet: The Transformation of Gay and Lesbian Life*. New York: Routledge.

Seidman, Steven. 2016. *Contested Knowledge: Social Theory Today*, 6th edition. New York: Blackwell.

Seidman, Steven and Jefferey Alexander (ed). 2001. *The New Social Theory Reader: Contemporary Debates*. New York: Routledge.

Shaw, Clifford R. and Henry D. McKay. 1942. *Juvenile Delinquency and Urban Areas*. Chicago, IL: University of Chicago Press.

Shaw, Randy. 2018. *Generation Priced Out: Who Gets to Live in the New Urban America?* Berkeley, CA: University of California Press.

Sheller, Mimi. 2014. "The New Mobilities Paradigm for a Live Sociology." *Current Sociology Review* 1–23.

Sheller, Mimi and John Urry. 2006. "The New Mobilities Paradigm." *Environment and Planning A: Economy and Space* 38(2): 207–226.

Silver, Christopher. 1997. "The Racial Origins of Zoning in American Cities." In *Urban Planning and The African American Community: In the Shadows,* edited by June Manning Thomas and Marsha Ritzdorf, 23–42. Thousand Oaks, CA: Sage.

Sims, David P. 2007. "Out of control: What can We Learn from the End of Massachusetts Rent Control?" *Journal of Urban Economics* 61(1): 129–151.

Skocpol, Theda. 1985. "Bringing the State Back In: Strategies of Analysis in Current Research." In *Bringing the State Back In*, edited by P. B. Evans, D. Rueschemeyer, and T. Skocpol, 3–38. Cambridge: Cambridge University Press.

Smith, Michael Peter and Luis Eduardo Guarnizo. 2009. "Global Mobility, Shifting Borders and Urban Citizenship." *Community Studies and Development* 100: 610–622.

Smith, Neil. 1996. *The Urban Frontier. Gentrification and the Revanchist City*. New York: Routledge.

Soifer, Steven. 1990. "The Burlington Community Land Trust: A Socialist Approach to Affordable Housing." *Journal of Urban Affairs* 12(3): 237–252.

Somers, Margaret R. and Fred Block. 2005. "From Poverty to Perversity: Ideas, Markets, and Institutions over 200 Years of Welfare Debate." *American Sociological Review* 70(2): 260–287.

Stearns, Janet. 1988. "The Low Income Housing Tax Credit: A Poor Solution to the Housing Crisis." *Yale Law Review* 6: 203–228.

Sternlieb, George. 1966. *The Tenement Landlord*. New Brunswick, NJ: Rutgers University Press.

Sweeney, Robert E. 1968. "King Cotton's Dwindling Empire." in Federal Reserve Bank of Atlanta, *Economic Review* 53(2)2: 6–9. https://fraser.stlouisfed.org/title /884/item/34863/toc/298108.

Teresa, Benjamin. 2019. "New Dynamics of Rent Gap Formation in New York City Rent Regulated Housing: Privatization, Financialization, and Uneven Development." *Urban Geography* 40(10): 1399–1421.

The NeoGeorgist. 2019. "What is Under Heaven Belongs to All" Medium. https:// medium.com/@theneogeoist/what-is-under-heaven-belongs-to-all-d09b1eb1 877c.

Tighe, Rosie and Elizabeth Mueller (ed). 2013. *The Affordable Housing Reader*. New York: Routledge.

Torpey, John. 2018. *The Invention of the Passport: Surveillance, Citizenship and the State*, 2nd edition. Cambridge: Cambridge University Press.

Trounstine, Jessica. 2018. *Segregation by Design: Local Politics and Inequality in American Cities*. Cambridge: Cambridge University Press.

Tusell, Maria Sisternas. 2017. "Affordable Housing in Europe: Innovative Public Policies that can Effectively Address the Housing Crisis" Notes: Interacionals, Barcelona Centre for International Affairs, 1–16.

U.S. Department of Commerce, Bureau of the Census, Current Population Reports, 1950, 1970, 1980.

United States Fact Sheet: Federal Rental Assistance. 2019. Center on Budget and Policy Priorities. https://www.cbpp.org/sites/default/files/atoms/files/4-13-11hous-US.pdf.

US Census. Historical Census of Housing Tables: Home Values. https://www.census .gov/data/tables/time-series/dec/coh-values.html.

US Department of Housing and Urban Development. 2019. "Community Land Trusts and Stable Affordable Housing." https://www.huduser.gov/portal/pdredge/pdr-edge-featd-article-110419.html.

US Department of Housing and Urban Development, Office of Policy and Development Research. 1995. "Public Housing: Image Versus Facts."

Vogel, David. 1986. *National Styles of Business Regulation: A Case Study of Environmental Protection*. Frederick, MD: Beard Books.

Von Hoffman, Alexander. 2012. "History Lessons for Today's Housing Policy: The Politics of Low-Income Housing." *Housing Policy Debate* 22(3): 321–376.

Wacquant, Loic. 2009. *Punishing the Poor: The Neoliberal Government of Social Insecurity*. Durham, NC: Duke University Press.

Warren, Elizabeth and Amelia Warren Tyagi. 2016. *The Two Income Trap: Why Middle Class Parents are Going Broke*. New York: Basic Books.

Weber, Max. 1946. "Politics as a Vocation." In *From Max Weber: Essays in Sociology*, edited by H.H. Gerth and C W Mills, 77–128. Oxford: Oxford University Press.

Weber, Max. 1966. *The City*. New York: Free Press.

Weber, Max. 1968. *Economy and Society*. New York: Bedminster.

Williams, Paulette. 2004. "The Continuing Crisis in Affordable Housing: Systemic Issues Requiring Systemic Solutions." *Fordham Urban Law Journal* Article 4, 31(2): 413.

Wilson, William Julius. 1987. *The Truly Disadvantaged: The Inner City, the Underclass, and Public Policy*. Chicago, IL: University of Chicago Press.

Wirth, Louis. 1947. "Housing as Field of Sociological Research." *American Sociological Review* 12(2): 137–143.

Yglesias, Matthew. 2012. *The Rent is Too Damn High: What to Do About It, and Why It Matters More Than You Think*. New York: Simon and Schuster.

Zeidal, Adam. 2010. "Affordable Housing: The Case for Demand-Side Subsidies in Superstar Cities." *Urban Lawyer* 42(1): 135–169.

Zilberstein, Shira. 2019. "Space Making as Artistic Practice: The Relationship between Grassroots Art Organizations and the Political Economy of Urban Development." *City and Community* 18(4): 1142–1161.

Zukin, Sharon. 2014. *Loft Living: Culture and Capital in Urban Change*. New Brunswick, NJ: Rutgers University Press.

Index

About the Author

Randolph Hohle is an associate professor of Sociology at SUNY Fredonia. His previous books include *Racism in the Neoliberal Era: A Meta History of Elite White Power* (Routledge, 2018), *Race and the Origins of American Neoliberalism* (Routledge, 2015), and *Black Citizenship and Authenticity in the Civil Rights Movement* (Routledge, 2013) and is the coauthor of the sixth edition of *The New Urban Sociology* (Routledge 2019). He lives in Buffalo, New York, with his wife and children.

www.ingramcontent.com/pod-product-compliance
Lightning Source LLC
Chambersburg PA
CBHW022320280326
41932CB00010B/1173